So, Why Ar[e] Rocks Red?

A Guide to the Magnificent Geology Surrounding Sedona
by Mike Ward

A portion of the proceeds from the sale of this book is donated to Sedona's Friends of the Forest

About Friends of the Forest Sedona

The Friends of the Forest, Inc. is dedicated to assisting Sedona's Red Rock Ranger District of the U.S. Forest Service in maintaining, protecting, and restoring the natural and cultural resources of forest lands for the enjoyment and use of present and future generations. The objective of this nonprofit, volunteer group is to work in partnership with the Red Rock Ranger District of the Coconino National Forest in tasks it does not have the manpower or the funds to accomplish on its own.

History

The Friends of the Forest is a unique organization formed in 1994 as an outgrowth of the Sedona Forum, *Building Partnerships with the National Forest*. The Friends of the Forest is a nonprofit and nonpolitical service organization. In fiscal year 2006, volunteer members of the Friends provided over 22,000 hours of service and provided over $30,000 in funding for supplies and materials for Red Rock Ranger District staff projects for which budgeted funds and/or man-hours were not available.

Approximately one-third of the Friends membership live in the Sedona area and actively give of their time. Others are not able to personally participate but their membership dues and donations are vital in helping the Friends to underwrite projects on the Red Rock Ranger District.

Primary Goals

The primary goals for the Friends of the Forest are:

- Help the Forest Service maintain its trails and cultural resources
- Reduce the environmental damage caused by increasing human impact
- Assist in education and improve communication with the community
- Enhance the forest experience for visitors and residents alike

If you are interested in becoming involved the with the **Friends of the Forest** or for more information about the **Friends**, you are invited to contact the Red Rock Ranger Station at (928) 282-4119 and also visit our web site at: http://www.friendsoftheforestsedona.org

Copyright © 2007 by Michael K. Ward
Second U.S. Edition May, 2006
Library of Congress Control Number: 2006931081
ISBN: 0-9747677-4-3

Published by Nueva Science Press
A division of MTR Worldwide Publishers, LLC
1814 North 74th Place
Mesa, Arizona 85207
480 629-5977

So, Why Are the Rocks Red?
A Guide to the Magnificent Geology Surrounding Sedona
by Mike Ward

Foreword

Anyone admiring the magnificent red rock formations surrounding Sedona must wonder how this beautiful landscape came to be. In my personal quest to find answers to this question, I found many excellent books and Internet websites full of detailed information on the theories of the geologic evolution of the area. The books and articles I read discussed in overly technical detail the complicated geologic processes involved, filled with jargon like plate tectonics, volcanism, reverse faulting, and erosion mechanics. A further impediment to my attempt to understand the area's geology was the complexities of the continuously shifting Earth's crust over the immense and incomprehensible scale of geologic time.

As I worked to understand how Sedona's red rocks came to be, a generalized and decidedly non-technical geologic story began to evolve in my head. I set out to write the story down in comprehensible terms that made sense to me. This publication is the result of those efforts.

This is the abbreviated version of Sedona's real geologic story. The technical details have been greatly simplified. The core of the geologic story is as accurate as an abbreviated version can be. Also, using literary license that may cause professional geologists to cringe, I refrained from using technical geologic terms, opting to use common descriptive words in their place.

The chapters are arranged chronologically. For the most part, the story unfolds as the reader drives eastward from Jerome on SR 89A, through Sedona and up Oak Creek Canyon. Within the chapters, each formation and geologic event begins with a section called *The Essentials*. This section lists pertinent information about the geologic formation or event, including where it can be best viewed.

In sharing this story with you, I would also direct your attention to the bibliography in the back of this publication, listing the helpful books and websites from which my account was derived. Two of the most useful books were <u>Sedona Through Time, Geology of the Red Rocks</u> and <u>The Verde Valley, A Geological History</u>, both written by a local geologist and educator, Wayne Ranney.

Acknowledgments

There are two individuals whom I would like to publicly acknowledge for their invaluable assistance in the creation of this book. I would like to thank my good friend, Carol Wirkus, for her review of the text from a lay reader point of view for general comprehension and for her excellent editorial assistance.

I would like to also thank author, educator and geologist, Wayne Ranney, for his expert assistance with the geological facts in this book. Without Carol's and Wayne's valuable assistance, this book would not be possible.

A special thanks to Christopher Scotese of the PALEOMAP Project for allowing me to use several of his plate tectonic images. His work can be viewed at http://www.scotese.com.

The age estimates of the sedimentary rock layers throughout Arizona are constantly being redefined as rock dating technology improves. The rock layer age estimates used in this book are taken from Allyson Mathis and Carl Bowman as published in "What's in a Number", *Nature Notes*, Grand Canyon National Park, Volume XXI, Number 2, Spring 2005.

Mike Ward
September, 2006

Introduction
So, Why are the Red Rocks Red?

The red color in Sedona's sandstone is due simply to rust. A very thin film of oxidized iron coats each grain of quartz sand in the sandstone formations around Sedona. This iron oxide is a powerful coloring pigment. Just a very small amount can produce vivid colors in soils and rocks. Although red is the most common color, not all iron oxides are red. Some are brown, yellow, black or even green.

Sedona's sandstone originates from the breakdown of the granite rocks that formed the Ancestral Rocky Mountains, once located where the Rocky Mountains are today. Granite is comprised of minerals that contain some iron, but these minerals are generally green or dark brown. As the iron-bearing minerals react with oxygen and water, red iron oxide is created and forms a very thin, paint-like coating on the quartz sand grains. Over millions of years, the loose sand grains are compressed and cemented into the rock called sandstone.

The area's limestones are normally a light gray colored rock. The pink to red coloration of the Fort Apache Limestone above Sedona and the Redwall Limestone beneath Sedona is a result of the red iron oxide in the sandstone layers above it. Water leaches the iron oxide out from the sandstone formations. As the iron oxide rich water passes over the exposed limestone, the dissolved iron oxide stains the rock red.

The Schnebly Hill Sandstone Formation above Sedona

How Do Geologists Know How Old the Rocks Are?

The geologists who study and date rock formations use two dating techniques to determine the age of a specific rock layer, relative dating and absolute dating. Relative dating establishes the sequence in which the rocks were deposited but does not provide the exact age. Absolute dating techniques are able to determine the length of time the rock has been in place since it was formed.

Relative dating follows the "Rule of Pancakes": the rocks at the bottom of a series of layers are the oldest and the rocks on top are the youngest. This sounds easy and it is in areas like the Colorado Plateau where the rock layers have been relatively undisturbed since they were deposited. In areas where the rocks have been faulted, folded, or overturned, the process requires a little detective work. Using the principle that sedimentary rocks are always deposited in flat horizontal layers, disturbed sedimentary rocks can be sequenced by observing each layer's relationship to those layers immediately in contact with it.

The fossil record is also useful in determining the relative age of rock layers. This is accomplished by examining the sometimes microscopic record of known "indexed fossils." Indexed fossils are specific organisms that were widespread but lived for only a short period of geologic time. By comparing the presence or absence of these indexed fossils in the rock layers, geologists can identify whether or not two distant rock layers were formed in the same geologic time period, but cannot determine their age.

Absolute dating involves radiometric-dating techniques. Radioactive isotopes have a constant rate of decay and lose half of their radiation over a known period of time. This decay process is commonly known as a radioactive half-life. Radioactive isotopes begin to decay after they are crystallized within the rock. The known constant rate of decay of one of many different isotopes present in different types of rock provides the clock needed to calculate when a rock was formed.

Right: The Schnebly Hill Sandstone and Coconino Sandstone Formations in the upper reaches of West Fork

Chapter 1

Grasping the Scale of Geologic Time:
Putting it in Perspective

Geologic Time

The greatest obstacle to understanding the geologic story behind the rocks of Sedona is coming to grips with the very unhuman scale of geologic time. Our planetary system is roughly 5 billion years old. The Sun is thought to be about halfway through its life cycle. Toward the end of its life in another 5 or 6 billion years, when all its hydrogen has been consumed, the Sun will become a red-giant star enveloping all of the inner planets, including Earth.

From the analysis of moon rocks returned to Earth and tidal evidence discovered in some of the oldest rocks on Earth, scientists believe the moon was torn from Earth when a small planet-sized object smashed into the molten mass that was Earth about 4.5 billion years ago. Earth's surface is thought to have cooled enough for the crust to form shortly (relatively speaking) after the impact. In addition to creating the moon, this impact also tilted Earth's axis resulting in the changing seasons.

In our local area, geologists believe the lava rock of Mingus Mountain was formed some 1.8 billion years ago. The red rocks around Sedona were deposited 280 to 275 million years ago. The landscape around Sedona was later sculpted by 80 million years of erosion to its present form.

The nearly incomprehensible magnitude of these numbers and the enormity of geologic time, typically presented as shown on the following page, beg the question, how can all of this be put into some understandable and humanly scaled perspective?

A Humanly Scaled Geologic Calendar

Imagine dividing geologic time into a 12-month geologic calendar as depicted to the far left on the geologic time scale on the following page. The very beginnings of the formation of Earth's crust are set to the first moment of New Year's Day, and the present moment set to the last clock chime signaling midnight of the following New Year's Eve.

Each month of that calendar would approximate 365 million years. Each day of that geologic calendar would represent 12 million years. An hour would represent the passing of 500,000 years. By using this geologic calendar to date events in Earth's formation, the volcanic rocks of Mingus Mountain would have been formed around August 3rd (1.8 billion years ago). The Schnebly Hill Formation around Sedona would have been deposited between noon December 8th and 2 a.m. on December 9th (280 to 275 million years ago).

For perspective, the formation of life began around February 14th on our geologic calendar (3.5 billion years ago). The dinosaurs disappeared on December 25th at 11 p.m. (65 million years ago). The first humans wandered into Arizona just after 11:58 p.m. on December 31st to hunt the great wooly mammoth (13,000 years ago). Sunset Crater, east of Flagstaff, was formed at 11:59:53, seven seconds before midnight (980 years ago). And finally, Carl T. Schnebly established the first post office in the settlement named after his wife, Sedona, less than one second before midnight in our geologic calendar.

Earth's Evolving Geography

Another obstacle to understanding Sedona's geology involves Earth's continually shifting geography. The land on which we stand is continually moving around Earth's outer surface. It also has periodically fallen miles below and raised miles above sea level through geologic time. It may be difficult to believe, but before being lifted to its present elevation above sea level, Sedona was approximately 12,000 feet below the ocean floor at 6 a.m. on December 25th on our geologic calendar (80 million years ago).

A Traditional View of Geologic Time

The months of the suggested Geologic Calendar are superimposed on the far left side of this illustration of the traditional view of geologic time.

The Holocene Epoch, the past 10,000 years, would be represented by a band on the right scale that would be approximately the thickness of this sheet of paper.

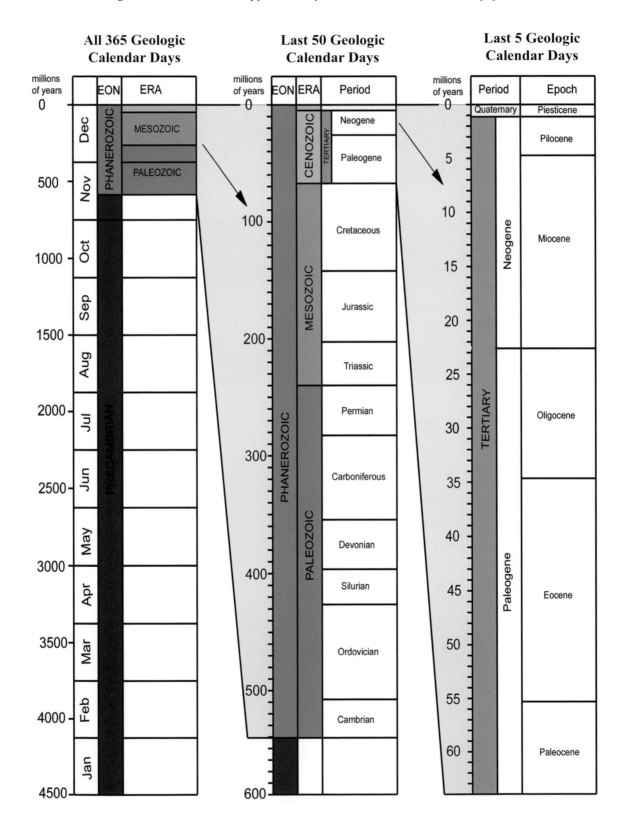

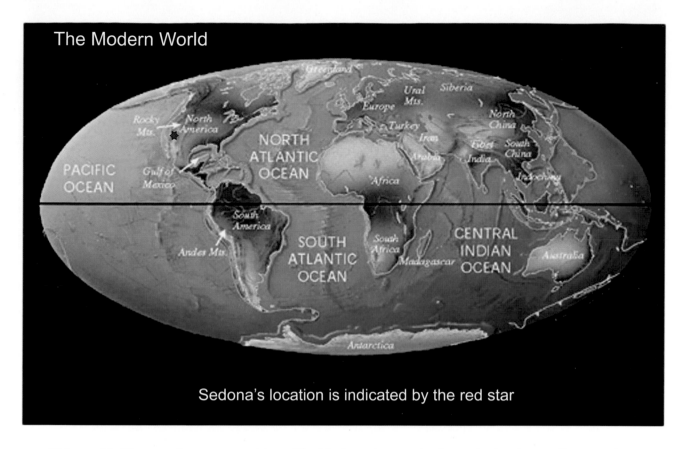

Sedona's location is indicated by the red star

This graphic illustrates the current position of Earth's dynamic tectonic plates. As the plates pull apart and once again collide, they will ultimately form a new supercontinent. (Christopher R. Scotese, PALEOMAP Project, http://www. scotese.com/Default.htm)

The mechanics of Earth's shifting surface were not known until the 1970's when scientists began to understand that the relatively lightweight, silica-rich, continental crust beneath our feet floats on the Earth's mantle like a bubbly froth on the surface of a simmering pot of soup. This now almost universally accepted theory of Plate Tectonics suggests that there are a dozen or so separate plates of continental crust that sit atop a heavier oceanic crust.

These individual plates move around the surface of the globe, periodically bumping into one another, creating mountain ranges and forming large supercontinents. These movements cause portions of Earth's crust to be raised above or sink below the seas. These supercontinents eventually break apart and move around to reform as new supercontinents.

Above is a graphic illustrating the present location of Earth's tectonic plates. Plate Tectonics graphics are used to help with the visualization of Sedona's past geographic location on the globe

during the story of Sedona's rock formation. The star shape ✦ represents the approximate location of Sedona on the Paleomap globe. These graphic images are reproduced courtesy of Christopher R. Scotese, PALEOMAP Project, http://www.scotese. com/Default.htm.

Sedimentation and The Role of Erosion

Perhaps the most important geologic process in creating the landscape around Sedona is erosion. Visitors mostly overlook the enormous influence of erosion in changing Earth's landscape. When Sedona's visitors are informed that Arizona was uplifted from below sea level, they often incorrectly visualize a great draining away of water exposing the present landscape. In fact, the magnificent formations around Sedona are the result of exposure to the sculpting forces of wind and water over millions of years.

The tectonic forces manipulating Earth's crust caused Arizona to be gently lowered below sea level over hundreds of millions of years. As the oceanfront real estate of Sedona dropped, layers of sandstone and limestone sediments were deposited and preserved. As the continental plate continued to drop below sea level, these sediment layers were protected from erosion. Eventually, Sedona lay buried more than two miles below the sea floor covered by over 12,000 feet of sedimentary rock formations.

The collision of the North American Plate with a small South Pacific Plate between De-cember 25th and December 27th of our geologic calendar (80 to 60 million years ago), caused the Southwest to be raised up over 3.5 miles and created the modern Rocky Mountains. The sedi-mentary rock layers thousands of feet thick, even miles thick, that had formed above Sedona were exposed to weathering and subjected to faulting from tectonic plate movement. The forces of wind, but mostly that of water erosion, have for the past 80 million years removed the sedimentary rock for-

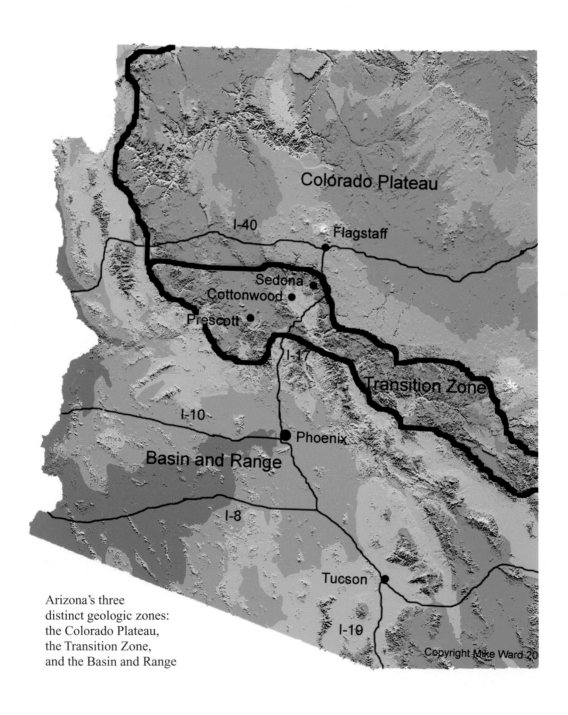

Arizona's three
distinct geologic zones:
the Colorado Plateau,
the Transition Zone,
and the Basin and Range

mations from above Sedona. This erosion process has continued to expose and sculpt all the red rock formations that make Sedona such a distinctive and beautiful place.

Only recently, geologists have recognized that the Grand Canyon, only two and a half driving hours north of Sedona, is a very young geologic feature. The canyon has been carved by a combination of the continuing, gentle uplifting of the Colorado Plateau and ongoing water erosion. The Grand Canyon has formed in the short geological span of 6 million years, only a half-day by our geologic calendar, scarcely the time the ancestors of modern man have been around. Such is the power of erosion.

As the rocks around Sedona continue their ceaseless battle with the forces of erosion, the Mogollon Rim above Sedona recedes further on its way toward Flagstaff. If left undisturbed by catastrophic tectonic plate events, the Mogollon Rim will eventually erode northward and merge into the Grand Canyon over the next tens of millions of years.

The Dynamic Rearrangement of the Earth's Surface

In reading the story of the rocks around Sedona, the reader may wonder why the beginning portion of Earth's story from early New Year's Day to late July of our geologic calendar is missing. The reason is that so much has changed in the evolution of Earth's surface that little or nothing remains of the early record for geologists to interpret. More than half of Earth's history is unknown. What is known from late July into early November is only fragmentary. Fortunately, the Black Hills and Mingus Mountain at least offer a glimpse of what happened in late July and early August around Sedona, and this information will be presented in the next chapter.

Around noon on December 30th, a much later tectonic event literally ripped Arizona apart along a line stretching from the northwest toward the southeast through the central part of the state. This faulting event cracked and rearranged the sedimentary rock deposits that covered the lower portion of Arizona. Sedona sits nestled beneath the Mogollon Rim, which is the northeastern edge of this great tearing, an area called the Transition Zone. This zone separates the relatively undisturbed northern slice of Arizona from the chaotically rearranged rocks of the southern portion of Arizona known as the Basin and Range.

It should be no surprise that the rock formations south and west of Sedona seem to be in the wrong location relative to how and when they were created. In fact, they have been violently rearranged. The story of these great deformation events will be explained in later chapters of this publication.

Paleontology, the Study of Ancient Life

The story of ancient life forms is important to understanding the geologic story of Sedona. Life forms contribute to the formation of sedimentary rocks. Coal, oil and peat are formed from decayed life forms. Limestones are formed from the skeletal remains of marine life forms.

The evolutionary story of life also aids in the visualization of the geologic story. For example, visitors often ask whether there are dinosaur fossils around Sedona. There are not any dinosaur fossils because the sedimentary deposits around Sedona were formed on December 8th of our geologic calendar (280 to 275 million years ago). Those deposits that would have contained dinosaur fossils are much later in age, ranging from December 14th to December 26th (200 to 65 million years ago). The dinosaur fossil-bearing deposits that would have been thousands of feet over Sedona are missing, having been completely eroded away.

Mass Extinction Events

The fossil record indicates to those who study ancient life forms, that life on Earth has undergone five major mass extinction episodes. Factoring in the many minor extinction events revealed in the fossil record, an extinction event has occurred with regularity approximately once every 26 million years.

With the exception of the famous K-T extinction event that ended the rule of the dinosaurs when Earth was struck by a giant meteor, scientists are not exactly sure of why the extinctions occurred. Theories on why this occurs range from periodic meteor bombardments, major volcanic eruptions, fluctuations in the heat radiation from our Sun, climate change, or perhaps all of these in combination.

Scientists have used the mass extinction events evident in Earth's fossil record to classify four major geologic eras.

■ **Precambrian Era** - The earliest of the geologic eras, the Precambrian Era dates from the formation of Earth to sometime mid-afternoon on November 16th of our geologic calendar. This Era covers nearly 90% of earth's history. Scientists believe the evolutionary story of life began somewhere around the 14th of February of our geologic calendar. As the chemistry of life slowly evolved, simple life forms had emerged by the end of the Precambrian Era

■ **Paleozoic Era** (Greek for Ancient Life)

o **Age of Marine Invertebrates** - Paleontologists date the Age of Marine Invertebrates as beginning at the end of the Precambrian period. This age lasted until a midday mass extinction event on November 25th in which about 85% of all life was lost.

o **Age of Fishes** -The extinction event gave rise to the Age of Fishes that lasted until early morning December 2nd when another mass extinction event claimed nearly 80% of all living species.

o **Age of Amphibians** -Then came the Age of Amphibians which ended around noon on December 11th with the largest of the mass extinction events, the Permian Extinction, in which 99% of all living species was lost.

■ **Mesozoic Era** (Greek for middle life)

o **Age of Reptiles** -Reptiles survived a mass extinction event in the early afternoon of December 14th only to be later ended with the famous K-T mass extinction around noon on December 26th. This event wiped out 75% of all life forms, ending the reign of the dinosaurs.

■ **Cenozoic Era** (Greek for recent life)

o **Age of Mammals** From the extinction of the dinosaurs to the present, is the **Age of Mammals**. Modern man finally came on the scene sometime around 11:45 p.n. December 31st (approximately 150,000 years ago).

Chapter 2

The Ancient Volcano: *Mingus Mountain, Jerome and the Black Hills*

(August 3rd and 4th, around 1.82 billion years ago.)

The Black Hills of Arizona dominate the horizon to the west of Sedona. At 7,880 feet in elevation, Mingus Mountain is the highest point of the Black Hills. Mingus Mountain can be easily located by looking for the cell phone towers on its crest. Nestled half way up the side of the Black Hills is the old mining town of Jerome, whose lights can be seen twinkling at night from many locations in Sedona.

The story of Mingus Mountain, the Black Hills and Jerome is interesting because if the Verde Fault had cracked Earth's crust a little further to the east or to the west, Jerome's story could have

been Sedona's, or conversely, Sedona's story could have been Jerome's. Through most of Earth's history, Jerome and Sedona shared the same geologic story. A faulting event only 10 million years ago, increased the distance between the two towns and radically changed how the two areas subsequently evolved into their present form.

The story of Mingus Mountain begins around August 3rd, some 1.8 billion years ago when Earth's land mass was joined into a supercontinent named Rodinia.

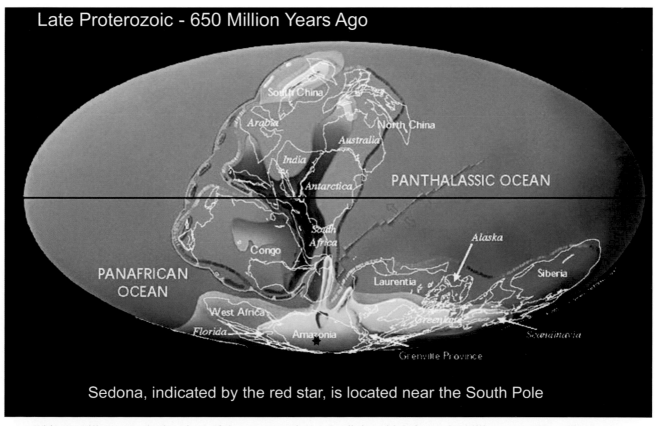

This map illustrates the breakup of the supercontinent, Rodinia, which formed 2 billion years ago. The Late Precambrian Era was an "Ice House" world, much like the present day world (Christopher R. Scotese, PALEOMAP Project, http://www.scotese.com/Default.htm)

Precambrian Rodinia

The volcanic activity that formed the ancient rock formation beneath Sedona took place as the oldest known supercontinent, Rodinia, was being formed. Rodinia existed in July and early August of our geologic calendar and included all or most of Earth's continental crust. Little is known of what preceded Rodinia or how it formed. The continental plate that is believed to have been the Ancestral North American Continent named Laurentia is located near the South Pole. Geologists believe Rodinia's entire land mass was clustered around Laurentia. As illustrated on the previous page, Sedona would have been located near the center of the Rodinia land mass at the South Pole.

The movements of the continental plates following the breakup of Rodinia are fairly well understood. Rodinia broke apart into eight large continents by late October. Australia and Antarctica separated from North America along a fault through the middle of Nevada and the western edge of Idaho. The continental crust would be later reassembled into another supercontinent called Pannotia and, after that, broken apart and again reassembled, as Pangaea.

Life forms had slowly evolved from their emergence as single-celled organisms into life forms that were more complex. As tectonic events formed Mingus Mountain in the last week of July (over 1.8 billion years ago), the oceans were populated with bacterium, aquatic algae and jellyfish.

The Volcanic Birth of Mingus Mountain

The Essentials

Formation:	The igneous rock below Sedona
Rock Type:	Rhyolite and basalt rock formed by molten magma
Time Frame:	August 3rd and 4th around 1.8 billion years ago
Era:	Precambrian
Life Forms:	Simple bacterium
Location:	Deep beneath the ocean near the center of the supercontinent Rodinia
Latitude:	Near the South Pole
Ave. Thickness:	Unknown
Best Viewed:	At the end of the road on top of Mingus Mountain. The Scenic Overlook above Jerome on SR 89A

Looking west from Cottonwood and Clarkdale

The foundation of Mingus Mountain and the Black Hills is comprised of some of the oldest exposed rock formations in the Southwest. These same rock formations underlay Sedona, which would be located very near Jerome if not for the faulting of the Verde Valley around noon on December 30th.

The land masses that would become the southern portions of Nevada, Arizona and New Mexico were small microcontinents that collided into the coastline of North America. The volcanic eruptions that created the rock formation beneath Jerome and Sedona were the result of the tectonic forces of these collisions. Well below the surface of the shrinking ocean caught between these land masses, hot magma welled up through cracks in the ocean floor depositing lavas of silica-rich rhyolite. These volcanic deposits were named the Deception Rhyolite after the Deception Gulch where they are found above Jerome along SR 89A.

Rhyolite is a cousin of granite. When silica-rich magma is deposited near the surface of Earth, rhyolite is formed. When this same material forms at a depth of more than three miles beneath the surface of Earth, the concentrated forces of heat and pressure form granite.

Alternating eruptions of rhyolite in Deception Gulch and another less silica-rich basalt five miles to the south of modern day Jerome resulted in alternating layers of cooled basalt and rhyolite as the vents intermittently expelled molten magma.

Eventually, a broad volcanic dome rose 2,000 feet above the ocean floor before the volcanic activity temporarily stopped. Small hot spring vents, known as black smokers, carried dilute liquid copper, gold and silver from the depths of Earth's mantle. The sudden cooling and drop in pressure caused the metal minerals to precipitate onto the ocean floor.

At some later point, continuing shifting plate activity caused molten magma to again rise up swelling this massive dome like a blister. In a cataclysmic explosion, pieces of rock and crystallized quartz were violently spread large distances over the ocean floor. Succeeding major eruptions formed

Mingus Mountain
elevation 7,780 feet

Mingus Mountain (right center) and the Black Hills viewed from
SR 89 near Cottonwood

layers of the volcanic ash exceeding 2,000 feet in thickness around the collapsing dome. This volcanic ash is known as the Cleopatra Crystal Tuff, named after Cleopatra Hill above Jerome where the tuff is visible surrounding the letter 'J.'

Following each eruption, the top of the dome buckled further into the void created in the magma chamber. Eventually the resulting collapsed dome formed a caldera exceeding a diameter of eight miles.

A view of the colorful rhyolite formations from above the Scenic Overlook on SR 89A above Jerome

The final volcanic chapter of the formation of Jerome's and Sedona's underlying foundation was the intrusion of crystallized basalt into the old collapsed volcanic dome. By the end of July of our geologic calendar, the volcanic activity around Jerome and Sedona finally came to rest.

Then a process called accretion compressed the Jerome area. Accretion involves the accumulation of many microcontinents colliding together in a manner similar to the way the "island arcs" of Japan and the Philip-

The letter "J" was placed in the Cleopatra Tuff volcanic ash created from the formation of the Mingus Mountain Volcano on Cleopatra Hill located above Jerome

Jerome's Copper Mining History

Copper-rich hot spring solutions laced with gold and silver continued to find their way up through small vents around the periphery of the eight-mile diameter caldera. Concentrated layers of copper sulfides and copper sulfates were deposited around the edge of the caldera. These copper deposits would later make the town of Jerome famous. The copper, gold and silver mined beneath Jerome are the oldest known mineral deposits in Arizona. In its heyday, the smelter below Jerome in Clarkdale produced over 4 million pounds of copper a month. The smelter also processed more than 50 tons of gold and 2,000 tons of silver as by-products during its 40-year history of smelting Jerome's copper!

A 2,700 lb. chunk of copper silicate from Morenci, AZ, called chrysocolla, containing Azurite and Malachite like that found beneath Jerome

pines are slowly pushing into Asia today. The accretion of the island arcs colliding with Laurentia caused intensive compressional northward pressure that deformed and crumpled the old volcanic dome into folds. These folds are in excess of 6,000 feet in height. This compressional process caused the sea floor around Jerome and Sedona to be uplifted thousands of feet. Eventually the accreted land masses added Nevada, southern Arizona and New Mexico to what would become North America.

Arizona's Jerome State Historic Park has many interesting displays about the geology beneath the town. Celebrating the half-century of mining and smelting copper, which ended in 1953, the museum is housed in the adobe mansion built for the Douglas family in 1914. The Douglas family owned the Little Daisy Mine in Jerome in which some of the highest grades of copper ore in the Americas were found. Some of the deposits assayed at almost 60% copper. The museum also has an excellent display of mineral rocks found in Arizona. The mining operations beneath Jerome cannot be truly appreciated until viewing the museum's three-dimensional model showing Jerome on the surface, the ore deposits, and the one hundred miles of tunnels going down 4,800 feet.

Pictured above is the old Douglas family mansion that became the Jerome Historic State Park.
Behind and below the museum lies the Verde Valley and in the distant background
is the Mogollon Rim that marks the edge of the Colorado Plateau.

Chapter 3

The Great Unconformity: *What's Not There and Why*
(August 2nd to November 19th, approximately 1.2 Billion Years)

The Great Unconformity

The Essentials

Formation Name: The Great Unconformity
Rock Type: Probably sedimentary rock
Time Frame: August 2nd to November 19th, 1.2 billion years ago.
Era: Precambrian
Life Forms: Aquatic algae and jellyfish
Location: Near the center of the supercontinent Rodinia
Latitude: Moving northward toward the equator
Ave. Thickness: Unknown
Best Viewed: The open pit mine behind Jerome's firehouse
Looking west from Cottonwood and Clarkdale

An unconformity is a gap in the rock records. These time gaps are caused when formations on Earth are deposited and then eroded away. A rock layer above an unconformity may be millions or even billions of years younger than the older rock layer immediately below it.

The entire rock record for August, September, October and half of November of our geologic calendar is missing in Arizona. This 1.2 billion year absence of rock in the geologic record is known as the Great Unconformity.

There are, however, sedimentary rock layers from this unconformity period preserved north of the Grand Canyon. From these rock records, geologists can reasonably infer what may have happened in Arizona.

The Great Unconformity represents over 1300 million years of sedimentary rock that is missing from Earth's geologic rock record. Those missing rocks were formed, eroded away multiple times before the Tapeats Sandstone was preserved in direct contact with the much older Precambrian Igneous rocks

Chapter 4

The Slopes of Jerome and the Cliffs of the Verde Canyon:
Tapeats, Martin, and Redwall Formations
(November 18th to December 5th, 525 to 320 Million Years Ago)

The Rock Formations Beneath Sedona

Located at 4,500 feet above sea level, Sedona is built on the remains of the relatively soft Hermit Shale Formation. Below the Hermit Shale and the other visible rock formations around Sedona, are over 2,000 feet of sedimentary layers of sandstone and limestone. In order to fully understand the geologic story of the formations surrounding Sedona, it is necessary to consider what is underneath and how it was formed.

Because millions of years ago, the movement of the Verde Fault caused the floor of the Verde Valley to drop thousands of feet, the sedimentary rock formations below Sedona are partially exposed along the slopes of the valley. The most impressive view of these formations are in the walls of the Verde Canyon through which the Verde River flows into the Verde Valley. Visitors can easily view these formations on an excursion through the canyon from Clarkdale to Perkinsville on the Verde Canyon Railroad.

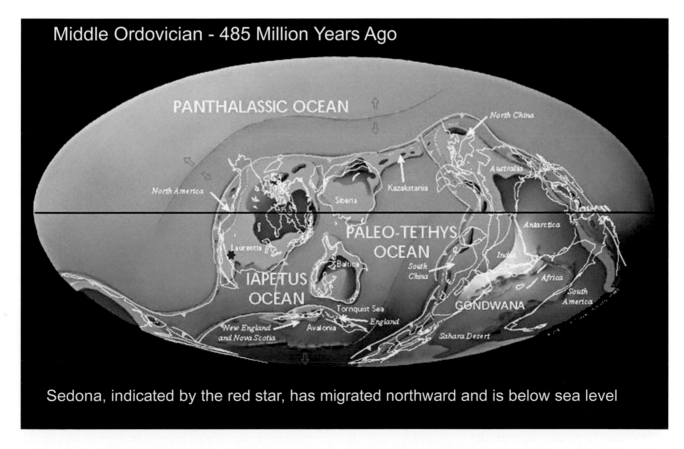

Ancient oceans separated the barren continents of Laurentia, Baltica, Siberia and Gondwana. This was one of the coldest times in Earth history. Ice covered much of the southern region of Gondwana. (Christopher R. Scotese, PALEOMAP Project, http://www.scotese.com/Default.htm)

What is Sedimentary Rock?

The oldest sedimentary rock in Arizona is the Tapeats Sandstone Formation. This sandstone formation was deposited beginning in the morning hours of November 18th (525 million years ago).

Sedimentary rocks are usually sandstones and limestones that were formed at or slightly below sea level. To be preserved, these deposits must be covered by successive formation deposits and be covered for long periods by seawater for protection from erosion. A simple way to think about it is to visualize these deposits being progressively layered down along a seashore at approximately the same rate as the continental plate is dropping below sea level.

Sandstone is formed as fine grains of quartz, feldspar, and other materials are blown in by the wind to form sand dune beaches near sea level. As the continental plate lowers, the tides come in and rework the sand dunes into horizontal layers. Over time, the actions of the water and the compression caused by the weight of overlaying sedimentary deposits form sandstone sedimentary rock.

Limestones are formed in shallow sea environments. As marine animals die, their calcium skeletons sink to the sea floor and are eventually cemented together. Limestones are generally uniform in consistency without the stratified banding commonly found in sandstones.

Sandstone and limestone deposits may be interlayered in a rock formation as the seas rise and fall along the shoreline during its creation. Rivers washed down other types of deposits, such as siltstones, mudstones, and conglomerates (rock and gravel cemented by limestone) that are intermingled within the sandstone and limestone formations. These combinations of sedimentary materials are the fingerprints geologists use to identify sedimentary rock formations. Rock formations are classified into distinct layers by their chemical and physical characteristics. As discussed previously on page 6, scientist can also date sedimentary rocks using both relative and absolute dating techniques to create a time chronology and, as one would assume, the youngest undisturbed layers are atop the older layers.

The Tapeats Sandstone Formation as viewed thousands of feet below Jerome along the Verde River near Sycamore Canyon. The Great Unconformity of 1.2 billion years separates the Tapeats Sandstone from the Martin Limestone

Tapeats Sandstone

Hickey Basalt

The Tapeats Sandstone Formation exposed above the open pit mine
as viewed from the Jerome Historic State Park

Tapeats Sandstone Formation (6 a.m. November 18th to 8 a.m. November 20th, 525 to 500 million years ago)

The Essentials

Formation Name:	Tapeats Sandstone Formation
Rock Type:	Sedimentary sand deposits
Time Frame:	6 a.m. November 18th to 8 a.m. November 20th, 525 to 500 million years ago
Era:	Early Paleozoic, Age of Marine Invertebrates
Life Forms:	Mollusks, brachiopods and trilobites
Location:	Coastal shoreline of an island continent off Gondwana
Latitude:	Near the equator
Ave. Thickness:	300 feet
Best Viewed:	The open pit mine behind Jerome's firehouse
	Looking west from Cottonwood and Clarkdale
	The Verde Canyon Railroad Milepost 29

The younger 525 to 500 million year old Tapeats Sandstone Formation sits directly on top of the much older 1.8 billion year old volcanic deposits that formed Mingus Mountain. The gap between the two formations is termed the Great Unconformity. The Tapeats Sandstone Formation can be seen high in the rocks above Jerome. For reasons that will be discussed in a later chapter about the formation of the Verde Valley, the same Tapeats Sandstone Formation can also be viewed thousands of feet lower in elevation for a short distance along the banks of the Verde River west of Sycamore Canyon. Beyond that point in the Verde Canyon, the Tapeats Sandstone Formation is beneath the bottom of the canyon floor.

The Tapeats Sandstone Formation was formed in the middle of November of our geologic calendar, during the Age of Invertebrates. Life had not yet encroached upon dry land. The seas were full of marine animals with hard external skeletons, including

21

Blocks of Tapeats Sandstone Formation used in the construction of buildings
throughout Jerome

mollusks, brachiopods and trilobites. At this time, the Sedona area was an arid, expansive, low-lying and featureless shoreline on an island continent off Gondwana near the equator. The shoreline extended from what is now Mexico to Canada. The land masses that formed what are now California, Oregon and Washington would be accreted onto the North American Plate at a much later date.

Outcrops of the Tapeats Sandstone Formation can be found as far north as Montana. To the south of Arizona's Black Hills, the Tapeats Sandstone Formation, and nearly all the subsequent formations that can be found in northern Arizona, have been largely eroded away. This erosion was the result of southern Arizona being crumpled by a much later tectonic plate expansion event forming the Basin and Range Zone.

Blocks of the Tapeats Sandstone Formation were used in the construction of many of the old historic buildings in Jerome. The distinctive dark, red-brown sandstone easily identifies these buildings.

The Martin Limestone Formation (Midnight to Noon on November 29th, 385 to 380 million years ago)

The Essentials

Formation Name: Martin Limestone Formation
Rock Type: Marine deposited dolomite limestone
Time Frame: Midnight to Noon November 29th, 385 to 380 million years ago
Era: Paleozoic, Age of Fishes
Life Forms: Horsetails and ferns; sharks, ammonites and giant sea scorpions
Location: Deep beneath the ocean an island continent off Gondwana
Latitude: Near the equator
Ave. Thickness: 200 to 800 feet
Best Viewed: Along the Verde Canyon Railroad
                 The tunnel near Milepost 22

The time gap between November 20th and November 29th, spanning approximately 165 million years, between the formation of the Tapeats Sandstone Formation and Martin Limestone For-

The 680 foot long tunnel cut through Martin Limestone on the Verde Canyon Railroad

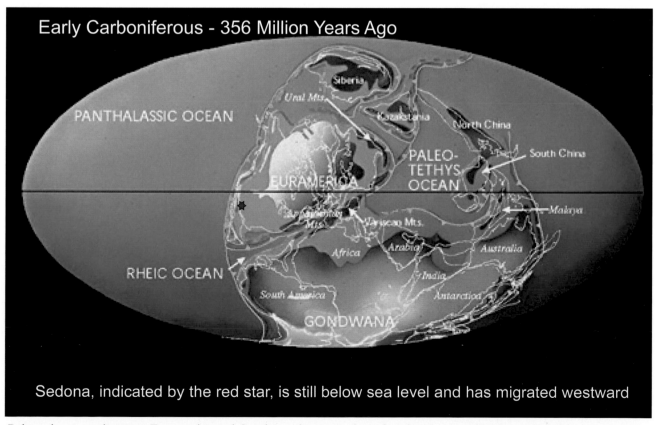

Paleozoic oceans between Euramerica and Gondwana began to close, forming the Appalachian and Variscan Mountains. (Christopher R. Scotese, PALEOMAP Project, http://www.scotese.com/Default.htm)

mation, is another unconformity. Sedimentary layers formed during this unconformity can be found in Utah and Nevada but are absent in Arizona. This unconformity was probably the result of Arizona having been above sea level where sediments could not collect and be preserved.

There were two mass extinction events during this unconformity period. The first mass extinction event on November 25th ended the Age of Invertebrates, to begin the Age of Fishes. Land plants had emerged in the form of scale trees, rushes, horsetails and ferns. The sea was populated with sharks whose teeth were the size of a man's hand, armored fish, ammonites and 10-foot long sea scorpions. Amphibians were just making their first appearance on land. The second mass extinction on December 1st would end the Age of Fishes and usher in the Age of Amphibians.

Following the 165 million year time gap, the 200 to 800 foot thick, Martin Limestone Formation was deposited. It was formed as the Sedona area was a shallow sea continental shelf environment at the beginning of the Age of Amphibians. The block-shaped deposits are comprised of dark gray limestone and dolomite containing many fossils of brachiopods and sponges. The formation is most visible along the banks of the Verde River through the Verde Canyon. The 680 foot long railroad tunnel on the Verde Canyon Railroad cuts through the Martin Limestone Formation on its way to Perkinsville.

The cliffs of the Redwall Limestone and Martin Limestone Formations in the Verde River Canyon along the Verde Canyon Railroad

The Redwall Limestone Formation (December 3rd to December 4th, 340 to 330 million years ago)

The Essentials

Formation Name: Redwall Limestone Formation
Rock Type: Marine-deposited limestone
Time Frame: Noon December 3rd to noon December 4th, 340 to 330 million years ago
Era: Paleozoic, Age of Fishes
Life Forms: Horsetails and ferns; sharks, ammonites and giant sea scorpions
Location: Shallow tropical seas near an island contnent off Gondwana
Latitude: Near the Equator
Ave. Thickness: 350 feet
Best Viewed: Along the Verde Canyon Railroad Above the Phoenix Cement Plant in Clarkdale

The Redwall Limestone Formation is important to the residents and visitors of Sedona because that is where they obtain their water. Aquifers passing through the Redwall Limestone nearly 1,000 feet below Sedona carry water from below the Colorado Plateau to where the water eventually emerges through springs to feed Oak Creek, as well as the Verde River and its tributaries.

As with the Tapeats Sandstone Formation, the 350 foot thick Redwall Limestone Formation was deposited over the entire Southwest as far north as Montana between December 3rd and 4th. When this limestone was formed, southwestern North America was a shallow, tropical sea located near the equator. This sea was populated with numerous marine animals including bryozoans, nautilus and corals, whose calcium remains would form the

The Redwall Limestone Formation being quarried on the Yavapai-Apache Reservation
Phoenix Cement Plant in Clarkdale

Redwall Limestone Formation. The formation gets its name from its tendency to form near-vertical walls in the Grand Canyon, making it difficult to find passages down into the canyon.

The vertical Redwall Limestone Formation cliffs in the Verde Canyon are reddish to pink-gray color with a muddled texture. Although the water-soluble limestone is actually a light gray color, the observed reddish stain is the result of solutions of iron oxides that leached out from the red sandstone formations above and ran down the limestone cliff face. These iron oxide-rich solutions were absorbed into the exposed surfaces of the limestone.

The Phoenix Cement Plant, owned by the Yavapai-Apache Indian Tribe and located near Clarkdale, quarries the nearly pure limestone in the Redwall Limestone Formation. This limestone is perfect for the manufacture of Portland cement. The cement plant was built in the 1950's to supply the cement for building the Glen Canyon Dam near Page, Arizona.

At the end of the Redwall Limestone Formation period, Arizona began the transition from beneath a warm tropical sea to a low coastal flood plain. Many rivers flowing southwestward from the continent's interior to the retreating sea cut through this plain. As these rivers cut meandering channels through the limestone bed, gravels were brought down and deposited by the flowing river waters along the riverbeds. These deposits hardened into conglomerates and sandstones that are embedded in the upper layers of the Redwall Limestone Formation.

Unlike the solid red Supai sandstones above it, the limestone of the Redwall Limestone Formation is actually gray in color, as shown in this rock fall. This rock fall of Redwall Limestone covers the Martin Limestone Formation behind it just east of the entrance to the railroad tunnel in the Verde Canyon. The red stain on the Redwall Limestone cliff surfaces is from the iron oxide that leaches out of the Supai Sandstone above it.

Chapter 5

The Hills Along the Road to Sedona: *The Supai Group and Hermit Shale Formation*

(December 5th to December 8th, 315 to 280 million years ago)

The Supai Group

The Essentials

Formation Name: Supai Group
Rock Type: Primarily sandstone intermingled with limestone, mudstone and coastal siltstone
Time Frame: 6 p.m., December 5th to 6 a.m., December 8th, 315 to 285 million years ago.
Era: Late Paleozoic, Age of Amphibians
Life Forms: Giant amphibians and mammal-like reptiles
Location: Coastal plains, early Pangaea
Latitude: North of the equator

Ave. Thickness: 900 feet
Best Viewed: Along the Verde Canyon Railroad Beneath Midgley Bridge on SR 89A north of Sedona

The Supai Group overlies the Redwall Limestone Formation throughout most of the Southwest. The formation is called the Supai Group because geologists classify it into four separate layers. During the time the Supai Group was being formed, Pangaea was in its formative stage.

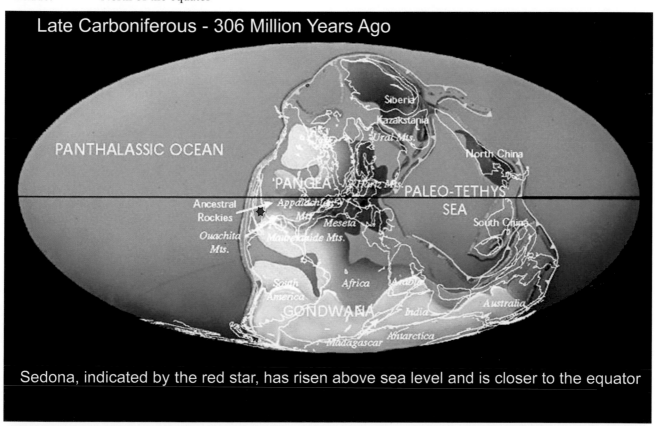

Late Carboniferous - 306 Million Years Ago

Sedona, indicated by the red star, has risen above sea level and is closer to the equator

By the Late Carboniferous period the continents that make up modern North America and Europe had collided with the southern continents of Gondwana to form the western half of Pangaea. Ice covered much of the southern hemisphere and vast coal swamps formed along the equator. (Christopher R. Scotese, PALEOMAP Project, http://www.scotese.com/Default.htm)

The Appalachian Mountains were being uplifted as the North American Continent collided with India and Africa.

This era is sometimes referred to as the Pennsylvanian Period because dense forests of large trees, conifers and ferns dominated what would be the eastern United States. These carbon-rich materials would later form the great coal fields in Pennsylvania. Animal life forms of this era included numerous varieties of amphibians, some of colossal size, and mammal-like reptiles.

Between midday of December 5th and December 6th, Sedona was located on the far western edge of the emerging supercontinent Pangaea. The

Above: The Supai Group below Midgley Bridge on SR 89A north of Sedona

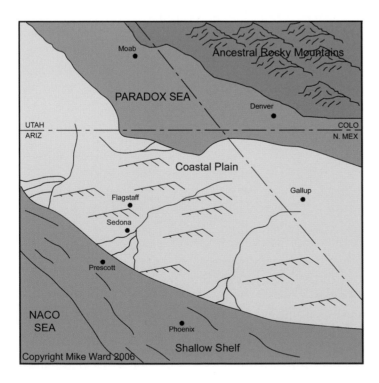

area was a low-lying desert trapped between a shallow sea to the northeast and a great ocean to the southwest. As the sea levels rose and fell, the land was alternately awash by tides or left dry and inhospitable. Imagine the flat, featureless, barren desert sands of today's Arabian Peninsula and that would be an accurate image of the land that would become Sedona.

The lower layers of the Supai Group are comprised of gray limestones from the retreating tropical seas. The upper layers of the Supai Group are comprised of red mud

Left : The Supai Group was formed when Sedona was located on a sandy coastal plain between the Paradox and Naco seas (adapted courtesy of Wayne Ranney, *Sedona Through Time*, 2001)

28

and coastal sands deposited on the coastal deltas. The difference between the two layers was caused as wind-deposited sand built up the coastal plain. The land was less subject to the encroachment of the seas and increasingly less limestone was deposited within the formation.

The Supai Group reaches a depth of over 300 feet in the inner gorge of Sycamore Canyon along the Sycamore Creek/Parson Springs Trail. Also, the red blockish Supai Group caps most of the canyon walls of the Verde Canyon between Sycamore Canyon and the railroad tunnel on the Verde Canyon Railroad. In the Sedona area, the Supai Group is exposed beneath Midgley Bridge on SR 89A just north of Uptown Sedona. The Supai Group is also exposed in the road cuts west of Sedona along SR 89A from the high school to FR 525 toward Cottonwood.

The transition between the Supai Group (below) and the Hermit Shale (above) .6 miles west of Upper Red Rock Loop Road at SR 89A. The basalt fills a joint in the Cathedral Fault

The Hermit Shale Formation

The Essentials

Formation Name: Hermit Shale Formation
Rock Type: Silt and mudstone
Time Frame: 4 p.m. December 8th, 280 million years ago
Era: Late Paleozoic, Age of Amphibians
Life Forms: Giant amphibians, and mammal like reptiles.
Location: Coastal river deltas of an emerging Pangaea
Latitude: North of the equator
Ave. Thickness: 300 feet
Best Viewed: Road cuts on SR 89A west of the post office near the "Y" in Sedona

By 6 p.m. on December 8th of our geologic calendar, 285 million years ago, a great mountain range located to the north and east of Sedona had been uplifted by a collision between the North American Continent and South America. This range is commonly known as the Ancestral Rocky Mountains because they were located in approximately the same location through Colorado and Wyoming as the current Rocky Mountains. Around midnight on December 8th, the Hermit Shale Formation was deposited over the Supai Group around Arizona and Utah.

The Hermit Shale Formation is comprised of sands and mud silt that flowed along the southwestward moving river systems, draining the great mountains and forming alluvial fans over the Supai Group lowlands of Arizona and Utah. Modern Sedona is built upon the eroded plains of the Hermit Shale Formation. These very soft mudstones and siltstones of the Hermit Shale Formation are responsible for the erosion that sculpted rocks that we see in Sedona today.

The tectonic forces that created the Verde Valley much later on the morning of December 30th would expose the Hermit Shale Formation. The easily eroded Hermit Shale Formation would then be eroded out from under the top-lying Schnebly Hill Sandstones, causing the rocks above to crumble under their weight. These rocks were broken up and carried away by wind and water, sculpting what is seen in Sedona today. The tall spires of Twin Buttes, Cathedral Rock, Bell Rock and Courthouse Butte survived this process. This was perhaps because the thinness and/or localized hardness of the Hermit Shale Formation under these formations was less subject to erosional forces.

The Hermit Shale Formation is mostly eroded away or rests below the soils of Sedona. There are outcroppings of the shale exposed in road cuts along SR 89A in West Sedona. One of the best locations to see the Hermit Shale Formation is in the road cut just west of the post office near the "Y" in Sedona.

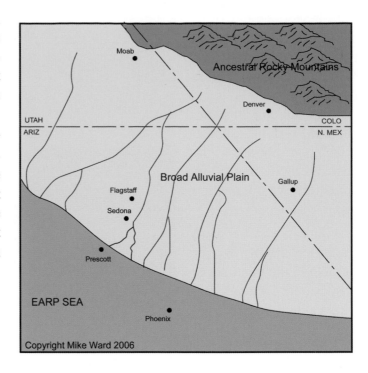

Above :The soft Hermit Shale was formed from deposits of silts and alluvial materials washed down by rivers (adapted courtesy of Wayne Ranney, *Sedona Through Time*, 2001)

The Hermit Shale Formation in the road cut west of the Sedona Post Office on SR 89A

Chapter 6

The Red Rock Landscape Around Sedona:
The Schnebly Hill Formation
(8 p.m. to 10 p.m., December 8th, 278-276 Million Years Ago)

The Schnebly Hill Formation

The Schnebly Hill Formation is uniquely localized around Sedona. The other sedimentary formations in Arizona are vast expanses of rock covering four or more states. The Schnebly Hill Formation extends along the base of the Mogollon Rim for only 20 miles. Named after Sedona's founders, Carl and Sedona Schnebly, it is the only formation in Arizona bearing a family name.

The primary reason Sedona attracts over 4 million visitors each year is the magnificent red rocks of the Schnebly Hill Formation. Whether visitors come for their unusual natural beauty, the artistic inspiration they instill, or soothing effect the red rocks have on the soul, they all leave knowing the uniqueness of the red rocks of the Schnebly Hill Formation.

There are three distinct layers or members of the Schnebly Hill Sandstone formation. They include the lower dark-red Bell Rock Member, the middle dark-gray Fort Apache Limestone Member and the topmost red to buff-colored Sycamore Pass Member.

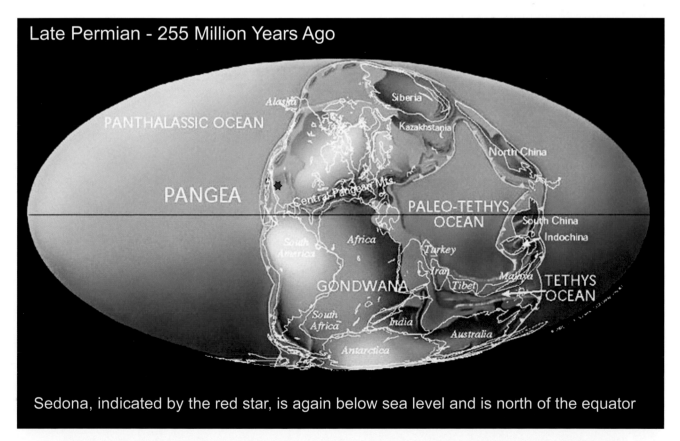

Sedona, indicated by the red star, is again below sea level and is north of the equator

Vast deserts covered western Pangaea during the Permian period, as reptiles spread across the face of the supercontinent. Nearly 99% of all life perished during the extinction event that marked the end of the Paleozoic Era. (Christopher R. Scotese, PALEOMAP Project, http://www.scotese.com/Default.htm)

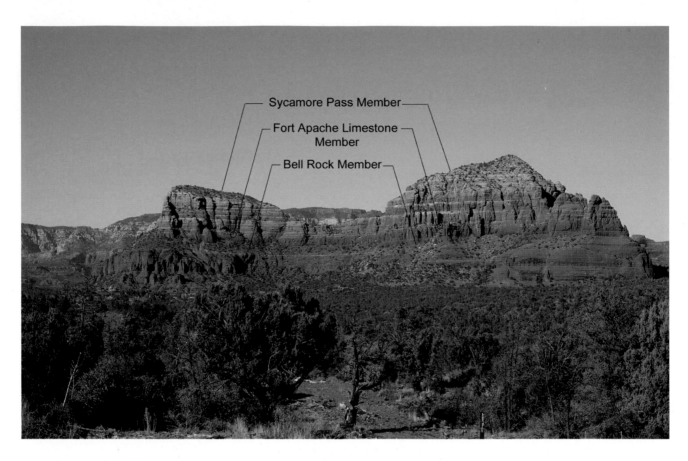

Twin Buttes: The Bell Rock, Fort Apache Limestone and Sycamore Pass Members of the Schnebly Hill Formation

The Coconino Sandstone Formation lies above the Schnebly Hill Formation on Capital Butte above West Sedona. The Fort Apache Limestone Member of the Schnebly Hill Formation becomes increasing thinner as it pinches out completely just north of Sedona.

The Bell Rock Member of the Schnebly Hill Formation forms the sloped sides of Bell Rock

The Bell Rock Member of the Schnebly Hill Formation

The Essentials

Formation Name:	Bell Rock Member
Rock Type:	Silt and sandstone
Time Frame:	8 p.m., December 8th, 278 million years ago
Era:	Late Paleozoic, Age of Amphibians
Life Forms:	Giant amphibians, and mammal-like reptiles.
Location:	Coastal dunes of an emerging Pangaea
Latitude:	North of the equator
Ave. Thickness:	500 feet
Best Viewed:	Bell Rock, Courthouse Butte, and Cathedral Rock Along SR 89A in Oak Creek Canyon to Milepost 380

The Schnebly Hill Formation was deposited as the Pedregosa Sea inundated the Sedona area and then retreated to the southwest (adapted courtesy of Wayne Ranney, *Sedona Through Time*, 2001)

As the supercontinent Pangaea was forming, the location of Sedona migrated northward from the southern latitudes to north of the equator, causing radical climatic changes that altered the landscape. Just after midnight December 9th (275-273 million years ago), great sand dunes were formed around Sedona as the sands of quartz, feldspar and other eroded bits of the Ancestral Rockies were blown in from the northeast across the Hermit Shale Formation. Near the end of the Age of Amphibians, this part of the world was a vast, desolate desert, devoid of terrestrial life forms. In appearance, this area probably resembled the present day Sahara Desert.

A large inland waterway named the Pedregosa Sea stretched across the southeastern portion of Arizona. Sedona was at the edge of the vast desert located on a coastal tidal plain at the northwestern extent of this sea. This was a period of a gentle lowering of the continental crust at almost the same rate as sand sediments were being deposited on the coastal plain. As the land lowered, the Pedregosa Sea repeatedly washed in over the coastal tidal zone. The newly deposited sands of the Bell Rock Member were constantly reworked by water as evidenced by the horizontal lines found in the lower portions of all the Schnebly Sandstone monuments around Sedona today.

The lower, 500-foot thick, Bell Rock Member Sandstone includes relatively large amounts of siltstone intermixed with the quartz sand. The clay binding material in siltstone causes the layer to erode with benches and slopes often called "slick rock." Bell Rock is comprised of this member of the Schnebly Hill Formation, giving this rock type its name.

The Fort Apache Member of the Schnebly Hill Formation

The Essentials

Formation Name: Fort Apache Limestone Member
Rock Type: Limestone
Time Frame: 9 p.m., December 8th, 277 million years ago

Era: Late Paleozoic, Age of Amphibians
Life Forms: Giant amphibians, and mammal-like reptiles
Location: Coastal dunes of Pangaea at the shallow end of the Pedregosa Sea
Latitude: North of the equator
Ave. Thickness: 10 feet in Sedona
Best Viewed: Merry-Go-Round Rock
Cap of Bell Rock
Saddle of Cathedral Rock

If you look carefully, you will notice that about two-thirds of the way up the sculpted rocks surrounding Sedona there is a very distinct thin band of rock that is colored differently than the red sandstones. This ten-foot thick layer is called the Fort Apache Limestone Member and was formed mid-morning on December 9th (272 million years ago). This was the time period when Sedona was submerged below the level of the Pedregosa Sea.

The Fort Apache Limestone caps Bell Rock and forms the well-known Merry-Go-Round Rock half way up Schnebly Hill Road. The Fort Apache Limestone also forms the saddle between the spires of Cathedral Rock at the end of Cathedral Rock trail.

The Fort Apache Limestone Member at Merry-Go-Round Rock halfway up Schnebly Hill Road

North and west of Sedona into the Secret Mountain Wilderness area off Dry Creek Road, the Fort Apache Limestone is "pinched out" and completely disappears. This absence marks the furthest extent of the encroachment of the Pedregosa Sea into Sedona. One hundred and thirty-seven miles to the southeast of Sedona near present-day Ft. Apache, Arizona, the Fort Apache Limestone is over 100 feet thick. As discussed previously, limestones are marine deposits comprised of the calcified remains of marine animals. The thickness of the limestone reflects the length of time a shallow sea covered the area.

The Bell Rock Member is softer than the Fort Apache Limestone Member. As the softer sandstone erodes and undercuts the limestone, large blocks of the Fort Apache Limestone break off and tumble down the sandstone slopes.

The Sycamore Pass Member of the Schnebly Hill Formation

The Essentials

Formation Name: Sycamore Pass Member
Rock Type: Fine grained sandstone
Time Frame: 10 p.m., December 8th, 276 million years ago
Era: Late Paleozoic, Age of Amphibians
Life Forms: Giant amphibians, and mammal-like reptiles
Location: Coastal dunes of Pangaea at the shallow end of the Pedregosa Sea
Latitude: North of the equator
Ave. Thickness: 200 feet
Best Viewed: Above West Sedona
The top of Twin Buttes
Top of Courthouse Butte
Spires of Cathedral Rock
Along SR 89A in Oak Creek Canyon
from Milepost 380 to the Junipine Resort

The spires of Cathedral Rock are formed by the Sycamore Pass Member. The Fort Apache Limestone Member forms the saddle of Cathedral Rock shown near the center of this view of the famous rock formation in Sedona.

Above the Fort Apache Limestone is the 200- foot thick Sycamore Pass Sandstone that was formed around noon on December 9th (272 to 270 million years ago). The sands creating the Sycamore Pass formation were deposited during a period when the continental plate was dropping more slowly than before. Because the sands were less frequently reworked by The Pedregosa Sea tides, great beach sand dunes were allowed to form.

A dropping of the continental plate finally allowed the Pedregosa Sea tides to rework the sands covering the dunes. As a result, the leeward surfaces of the dunes were preserved between the horizontal layers of water-worked sand, forming what is known as cross-bedding. These diagonally etched cross-bedded lines in the sandstone cliff walls make an interesting contrast to the horizontal banding of the water-worked sandstones above and below.

The Sycamore Pass Member has considerably less clay silt deposits than the Bell Rock Member. This causes the formation to erode into vertical cliffs, forming the tall spires found in Cathedral Rock for example. As the Pedregosa Sea retreated further to the south and east, the building sand deposits were increasingly less affected by the tides. The iron mixed in with the sand was less frequently oxidized by seawater. This resulted in more frequent cross-bedding of beige colored sandstone layers toward the top of the Sycamore Pass Member.

A black patina of desert varnish coats the Sycamore Pass Member of the Schnebly Hill Sandstone near the entrance to the West Fork Trail in Oak Creek Canyon (see chapter 11 for a description of desert varnish)

Chapter 7

The Cliff Walls Towering Above Sedona and Oak Creek Canyon:

The Coconino, Toroweap and Kaibab Formations

The Coconino Sandstone Formation

The Essentials

Formation Name: Coconino Sandstone Formation
Rock Type: Course grained sandstone
Time Frame: 2 a.m., December 9th, 275 million years ago
Era: Late Paleozoic, Age of Amphibians
Life Forms: Giant amphibians, and mammal-like reptiles
Location: Desert inland sand dunes of Pangaea
Latitude: North of the equator
Ave. Thickness: 600 feet
Best Viewed: The upper beige sandstones of Munds Mountain
The top of Capital Butte
The upper layers of Wilson Mountain above Uptown Sedona
Slide Rock State Park up Oak Creek Canyon
The lower cliffs at West Fork up Oak Creek Canyon

The 2,500 foot cliffs surrounding Sedona reach up to the 6,800 foot elevation of the Colorado Plateau. The most obvious formation above the red rock Schnebly Hill Formation is the beige-colored Coconino Sandstone Formation. On SR 89A up Oak Creek Canyon, at Slide Rock State Park, there is a good opportunity to view and walk in the Coconino Sandstone Formation.

There is no obvious transition line between the end of the Sycamore Pass Member of the Schnebly Hill Formation and the beginning of the Coconino Sandstone above it. Generally, the last evidence of a layer of red sandstone is considered to be the division between the two formations.

Once again, climate played a pivotal role in the shaping of Sedona's landscape. In the 85 million years between the deposition of the Redwall Limestone and the Coconino Sandstone Formation, the region was gradually changing from a wet tropical climate to an arid desert dominated by barren sand dunes.

The beige-colored Coconino Sandstone Formation of Munds Mountain is shown in the background behind Twin Buttes

As greater quantities of windblown, iron-free sands were deposited on an area comprising most of Arizona, Utah and western New Mexico, the Pedregosa Sea filled in, retreated southeastward, and eventually disappeared. Sedona was located in the center of a large inland sand dune desert, much like the Sahara Desert. The sand grains of the Coconino Sandstone Formation are substantially larger than the sand grains in the red sandstone layers below. Because of the larger grain size, water passes readily through the Coconino Sandstone Formation and any iron oxides leaching out from red sandstones that existed above the formation pass through the formation allowing it to retain its light sand color.

The 500-foot thick Coconino Sandstone Formation deposited through the afternoon and evening of December 9th is heavily cross-bedded. This cross bedding reveals that the leeward sides of the sand dunes are nearly always to the southwest. This indicates that the dunes continued their wind blown march in that direction for most of the five million years sand was deposited in the formation.

The distinctive cross-bedding and large grain size makes the sandstone ideal for flagstone. Along Interstate 40 are many quarries that supply the nation with large quantities of Coconino flagstone.

The Toroweap Formation

The Essentials

Formation Name: Toroweap Formation
Rock Type: White sandstone in Oak Creek Canyon Limestone and gypsum in Sycamore Canyon
Time Frame: 6 a.m., December 9th, 273 million years ago
Era: Late Paleozoic, Age of Amphibians
Life Forms: Giant amphibians, and mammal-like reptiles
Location: Shallow seas and desert inland sand dunes of Pangaea
Latitude: North of the equator
Ave. Thickness: 300 feet
Best Viewed: The upper reaches of the canyon walls at West Fork

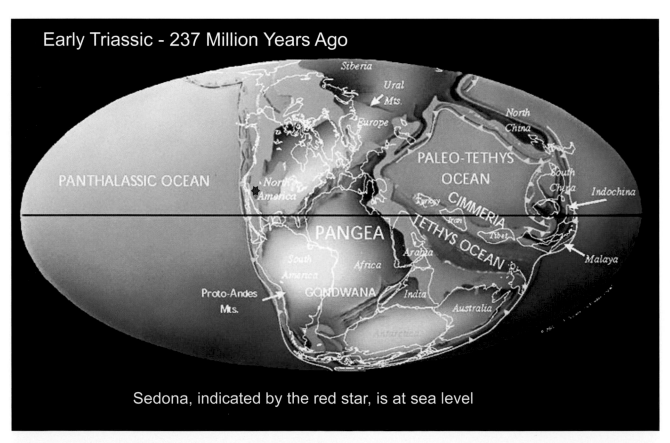

Early Triassic - 237 Million Years Ago

Sedona, indicated by the red star, is at sea level

The supercontinent of Pangaea, mostly assembled by the Triassic period, allowed land animals to migrate from the South Pole to the North Pole. Life began to rediversify after the great Permian Extinction and warm-water faunas spread across Tethys. (Christopher R. Scotese, PALEOMAP Project, http://www.scotese.com/Default.htm)

The lighter colored Toroweap Formation sandstone can be seen from Milepost 385 to part way up the switchbacks on SR 89A in Oak Creek Canyon. The transition from the Coconino Sandstone Formation to the Toroweap Formation is almost imperceptible. The subtle change in color and the different cross-bedding patterns are the main distinguishing characteristics between the two sandstones.

The Toroweap Formation that was deposited in the morning hours of December 9th was something of an enigma to geologists for many years. The Coconino-Toroweap Formation is an 800-foot thick formation of sandstone in Oak Creek Canyon. Further southwest, in Sycamore Canyon, the first 500 feet of the combined layers were deposited as inland and then coastal sand dunes. The top 300 feet were deposited as limestone under the encroaching Toroweap Sea.

Geologists theorize that the shallow Toroweap Sea covered western Arizona. Sands continued to be deposited on the coastline to the north and east but limestone was created under the shallow seas to the west. For now the two different sediment deposits are classified as one formation because they lie at the same elevation.

The Kaibab Formation

The Essentials

Formation Name:	Kaibab Formation
Rock Type:	Compositions of sandstone, limestone and chert
Time Frame:	December 9th, 270 million years ago
Era:	Late Paleozoic, Age of Amphibians
Life Forms:	Giant amphibians, and mammal-like reptiles
Location:	Deep sea to coastal plain of Pangaea
Latitude:	North of the equator
Ave. Thickness:	350 feet
Best Viewed:	One-half to one mile from the top of the switchbacks on SR 89A

As the land mass continued to drop, the Toroweap Sea advanced north and east covering most of Arizona and Utah. The deep-water environment covering Arizona promoted the growth of

The Coconino and Toroweap Formations looking north up Oak Creek Canyon from the top of Wilson Mountain. The San Francisco Peaks are in the background.

The Kaibab Formation in Oak Creek Canyon near Milepost 388 on SR 89A

sponges. During a five million year period, blooms of sponges came and died, raining massive amounts of silica needles down on the ocean floor to form the Kaibab Formation.

These silica deposits formed hard chert nodules in the limestones on the ocean floor. By shortly after noon on December 10th, the Toroweap Sea retreated as tectonic forces gently raised the land.

During this time period, Earth's climate began to heat up to become the hottest period in the history of the Earth. The cause of this climate change is unknown, but rainfall virtually ceased, land water disappeared, and most life forms on Earth died out. Known as the Great Permian Extinction, almost 99% of all living species vanished from Earth by noon on December 11th (245 million years ago).

There is fragmentary evidence for the continued creation of nearly 10,000 feet of additional sedimentary formations over the Kaibab Formation for another 10 million years. Then, following a great uplifting of the southwest, millions of years of exposure to wind and rain caused these layers to be eroded away. The primary characteristic that makes the Kaibab Formation so important was the formation of the hardened chert embedded in the sediment. This hardened chert made the Kaibab Formation very erosion-resistant and protected the layers below from further erosion. Without the Kaibab Formation, there would be no Colorado Plateau. Without the Colorado Plateau, there would be no Grand Canyon and there would be no red rock landscape around Sedona.

Chapter 8

Sedona Rising Up From the Ocean Depths: *the Laramide Orogeny and Carving the Red Rocks of Sedona*
(6 a.m. December 25th to 6 p.m., December 28th, 80-40 Million Years Ago)

The Laramide Orogeny

The Essentials

Event Name:	Laramide Orogeny (Mountain Building)
Event Type:	Uplifting of the Southwest
Time Frame:	8 a.m. December 25th to 6 p.m. December 28th, 80-40 million years ago
Era:	Late Mesozoic, Age of the Reptiles
Life forms:	Early primates and the great dinosaurs
Location:	Southwestern United States
Latitude:	North of the equator
Uplift:	Over 3 miles

On December 24th (80 million years ago), the Hermit Shale upon which Sedona is built today was approximately 15,000 feet below Earth's surface. On the surface, wet tropical forests were inhabited by the great reptilian beasts we call dinosaurs. The Pacific Ocean seacoast ran through the middle of Nevada. To the east, the great plains of North America lay under a shallow inland sea. The stage was set for two major events that would fundamentally change both the geologic geography of western North America and the evolution of life forms around the world.

Over several days of our geologic calendar (less than 40 million years), tectonic forces crushed a small South Pacific continental plate between the North American Plate to the east and the massive Pacific Plate to the west. The small Farallon Plate was pushed under the North American Plate, adding what is now California to North America and creating the Rocky Mountains. The entire western half of North America was uplifted approximately three miles during this time. The uplifting drained the mid-American inland sea

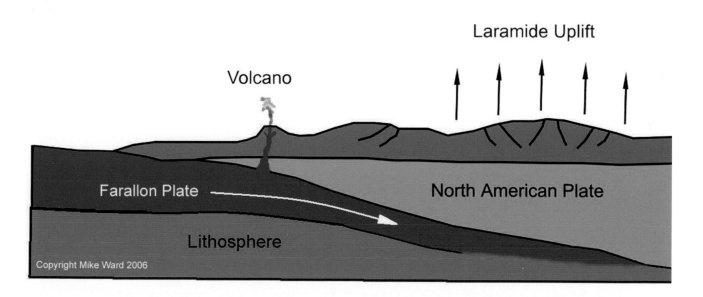

The North American Plate was uplifted over three miles 80 million years ago when the
Rocky Mountains were formed by the Laramide Orogeny

and raised Sedona from miles below sea level to its current location nearly a mile above sea level. This mountain-building event is known as the Laramide Orogeny.

To the north and east of Sedona, the land was uplifted as a block to form the Colorado Plateau. The sedimentary layers of this plateau were not greatly disturbed and remained locked in the horizontal strata we find today.

The North American Plate shifted a little to the south, riding up higher over the Farallon Plate to the south. The lands to the south and west of Sedona as far as Mexico were crumpled and distorted in another mountain-building event. These horizontal sedimentary layers were uplifted much higher than the Colorado Plateau and arched upward toward the southwest, causing them to crumble in massive broken blocks. This raised mountain land mass to the south and west of Sedona was named the Mogollon

Highlands. Phoenix was thousands of feet below the surface of these highlands.

The terrible forces involved in driving the Farallon Plate under North America and uplifting the North American land mass in such a relatively short geological time span was a period of cataclysmic earthquakes and violent volcanic activity. As the Farallon Plate made contact with the hot magma below North America, it was melted. The melted lightweight continental crust material was forced up faults in the North American crust and deposited by massive volcanoes and fault vents over the western United States. Most of the geologic record of this violent volcanic activity has been eroded away along with the sediments of the entire Mesozoic age of dinosaurs. However, the mountains of southern Arizona are the remnants of the volcanoes and metamorphic rock upwelling from this period.

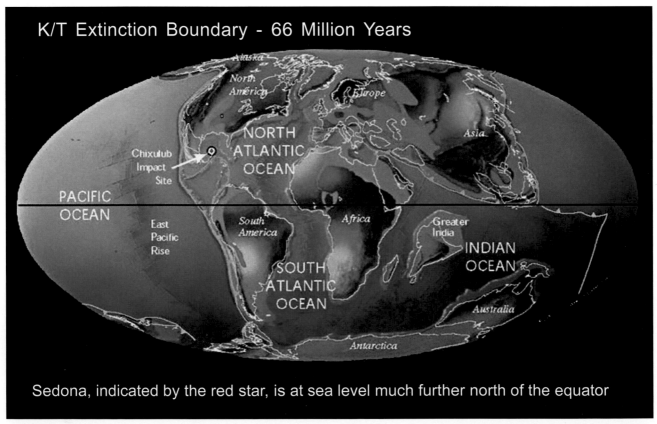

Sedona, indicated by the red star, is at sea level much further north of the equator

The bull's eye marks the location of the Chicxulub impact site. The impact of a 10 mile wide comet caused global climate changes that killed the dinosaurs and many other forms of life. By the Late Cretaceous the oceans had widened, and India approached the southern margin of Asia. (Christopher R. Scotese, PALEOMAP Project, http://www.scotese.com/Default.htm)

The K-T Extinction

Another cataclysmic event changed the entire world on December 26th (65 million years ago). The event was the impact in Mexico of a 10-mile wide comet causing global climate changes that killed the dinosaurs and 75% of other forms of life. This extinction event ended the reign of the reptiles and gave rise to the Age of Mammals and the eventual emergence of Man.

The Mesozoic Interlude

The Essentials

Event Name:	Mesozoic Interlude
Event Type:	Erosion of 10,000 feet of sedimentary rock from the Southwest
Time Frame:	Midnight December 26th to 6 a.m. December 28th, 60-40 million years ago
Era:	Early Cenozoic, Age of Mammals
Life Forms:	First land and sea mammals
Location:	North America forming from the breakup of Pangaea
Latitude:	North of the equator
Erosion:	Over 2 miles of material was erode away

As a giant rift in the Atlantic Ocean continued to grow, Pangaea was fragmented into the many continental masses with which we are familiar today. The uplifted lands of the Southwest were exposed to wind and water erosion. The entire 10,000-foot thick rock record for the 200 million yearlong Triassic, Jurassic and Cretaceous Periods of the Age of Reptiles and the great dinosaurs was worn away.

This unconformity of missing rock record is known as the Mesozoic Interlude, named after the era during which the great reptiles ruled the Earth. The dinosaur fossil-rich formations that once covered Sedona were entirely eroded away over the 40 million years between December 26th and December 28th.

The latest chapter in the geologic story of Sedona is the least well understood. There are several conflicting theories about how the geology around Sedona has evolved over the past 25 million years.

Looking down into Sedona from the saddle between Schnebly Hill and Munds Mountain

There were no witnesses to past geologic events. To understand the Earth's past, geologists are faced with the task of examining geological evidence, constructing a theory that best explains the evidence, and then testing the theory against new observations as they come along.

Ignoring the disputes over various details, the following presents a broad conceptualization of what probably happened following the uplifting of the Colorado Plateau and the Mogollon Highlands.

Crossbedded layers of gray to buff-colored Coconino Sandstone are clearly evident above the horizontal layers in the Schnebly Hill Formation, as viewed from Schnebly Hill Road.

Chapter 9

The Verde Valley Drops 6,000 Feet: *Volcanoes, the Creation of the Mogollon Rim and the Verde Formation*
(8 p.m., December 29th to Noon December 31st, 28 to 6 Million Years Ago)

The Ancestral Mogollon Rim

The Essentials

Event Name: Formation of the Ancestral Mogollon Rim

Event Type: Erosion of sedimentary rock down to the Hermit Formation

Time Frame: 10 p.m. December 29th to 8 a.m. December 30th, 25 to 20 million years ago

Era: Middle Cenozoic, Age of Mammals

Life Forms: First anthropoid apes and grasses

Location: Formation of the modern world

Latitude: North of the equator

Erosion: Cutting an erosional trough west of Sedona

Between 25 to 20 million years ago, the Colorado Plateau to the north of Sedona was still gradually uplifting without major disruption to the horizontal layers of rock. The broken up sedimentary layers of the mountains forming the Mogollon Highlands to the south and west of Sedona were subjected to severe erosion because of the progressively steep upward angle of the chaotic land surface. Eroded materials were quickly washed northeastward down the steep slopes and deposited as far north as central Utah.

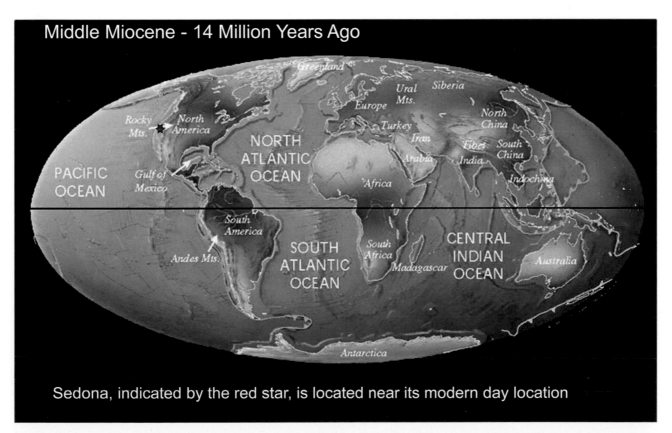

Middle Miocene - 14 Million Years Ago

Sedona, indicated by the red star, is located near its modern day location

20 million years ago, Antarctica was covered by ice and the northern continents were cooling rapidly. The world has taken on a "modern" look, but notice that the sea flooded Florida and parts of Asia. (Christopher R. Scotese, PALEO-MAP Project, http://www.scotese.com/Default.htm)

As erosion of the Mogollon Highlands continued, the river channels moving the eroded materials encountered harder layers of the gently rising Colorado Plateau. The rivers were deflected southward, moving toward the oceans to the south. The rivers started cutting a deep channel into the edge of the Colorado Plateau approximately where the Verde River flows today. Once the soft Hermit Shale was encountered, the waters quickly eroded it, undercutting the harder formations above the Hermit Shale. As the harder rocks crumbled into the forming canyon, the Ancestral Mogollon Rim was formed. The Mogollon Rim has been retreating northeastward for about 15 million years to its present location at the rate of nearly one foot every 600 years. This retreat of the Mogollon Rim above the erosion-prone Hermit Shale is responsible for the landscape around Sedona today.

The Hickey Formation and House Mountain Volcano

The Essentials

Formation Name: Hickey Formation and House Mountain
Rock Type: Volcanic Basalt
Time Frame: 2 p.m. to 10 p.m., December 30th, 15 to 6 million years ago

Era: Middle Cenozoic, Age of Mammals
Life Forms: First sign of early man and whales
Location: High desert basin of the modern world
Latitude: North of the equator
Ave. Thickness: Several hundred feet
Best Viewed: Along the top of Mingus Mountain and the Black Hills
House Mountain viewed from 89A and FR 525

Beginning about 17 million years ago, the tectonic compressional forces that uplifted and folded the Mogollon Highlands began to ease as the Farallon Plate disappeared under the North American Plate. With the release of the compressional pressure, southern Arizona began to extend in the same manner a piece of paper that bows up when pushed against an object on a tabletop and flattens out when the pushing force is released. This process formed what is now known as the Basin and Range Zone that curves upward through southern Arizona into Nevada.

The extension of the Basin and Range created many faults. The extension caused the faulted columns of sedimentary rock to fall over and slide southward in the same manner as a row of books on a shelf would fall and slide when the book-

House Mountain
elevation 5,127 feet

House Mountain Basalt viewed looking south from SR 89A near FR 525 between Sedona and Cottonwood

ends are removed. Magma seeped out from deep in the mantle through many of these faults, creating extensive lava flows throughout central and southern Arizona. For a period of 5 million years, magma intermittently flowed from Mingus Mountain and the other fault vents in central Arizona covering the area with huge flows of basalt lava. The lavas from Mingus Mountain formed the Hickey Formation visible on the top of the Black Hills to the southwest of the Verde Valley. The Rim Basalts to the north and east of the Verde Valley along the Mogollon Rim were formed much later, about 6 million years ago.

Between 15 to 13 million years ago, a massive shield volcano formed to the south of present day Village of Oak Creek. The volcano is named House Mountain because of the eroded house shaped basalt cap on the mountain top. The lavas from House Mountain primarily flowed south and westward into the Verde River drainage. The basalt flows from House Mountain are visible along SR 89A from Dry Creek westward toward Cotton Wood. The eroded remains of House Mountain volcano are easily seen from SR 89A and FR 525 looking toward the south.

The Creation of the Verde Valley

The Essentials

Event Name:	Formation of the Verde Valley
Event Type:	Normal faulting
Time Frame:	4 a.m to 6 a.m., December 31st 10 to 9 million years ago
Era:	Middle Cenozoic, Age of Mammals
Life Forms:	First sign of early man and whales
Location:	High desert basin of the modern world
Latitude:	North of the equator
Faulting:	The Verde Fault causes the floor of the Verde Valley to drop 6,000 feet

House Mountain Basalt near Milepost 363.5 on SR 89A between Sedona and Cottonwood

Photographed from the saddle of Cathedral Rock, this basalt has been dated from the same period as House Mountain. The basalt rose through a crack in the Schnebly Hill Sandstone Formation, passing through Cathedral Rock to form a small volcano in the center of the famous rock formation.

About 10 to 9 million years ago, the Verde Fault became active and the Verde Valley was expanded. The Verde Valley was already a large erosional valley undercutting the Ancestral Mogollon Rim between the Colorado Plateau and the Mogollon Highlands. As the southern portion of Arizona continued to be pulled apart, the Verde Fault shifted and the valley was down dropped as the Black Hills were uplifted exposing the ancient Mingus Mountain volcanic rhyolites.

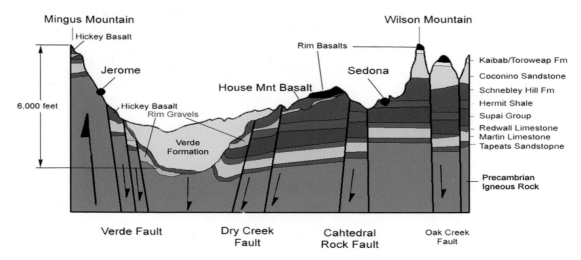

Mingus Mountain
Hickey Basalt
Jerome
6,000 feet
Hickey Basalt
Rim Gravels
Verde
Formation

Rim Basalts
House Mnt Basalt
Sedona

Wilson Mountain
Kaibab/Toroweap Fm
Coconino Sandstone
Schnebley Hill Fm
Hermit Shale
Supai Group
Redwall Limestone
Martin Limestone
Tapeats Sandstopne
Precambrian
Igneous Rock

Verde Fault
Dry Creek
Fault
Cahtedral
Rock Fault
Oak Creek
Fault

A schematic cross-section showing the faulting that formed the Verde Valley 10 million years ago. Notice that the Jerome side (Mogollon Highlands) of the fault was higher in elevation than the Sedona side (Colorado Plateau) of the fault before the Verde Valley was formed.

Evidence of the 6,000 foot displacement of down dropping and uplifting comes from core samples taken near Cottonwood. These samples reveal that the Hickey Basalt that caps the Black Hills above Jerome is nearly 2,000 feet below Cottonwood. During this faulting event, large slabs of Earth's crust slid downward into the dropping valley in a stair step fashion as the Black Hills were uplifted. This would explain why the Redwall Limestone is located below the much older Tapeats Sandstone on the slopes near the Phoe-

nix Cement Plant. This stair step faulting also explains how the Tapeats Sandstone Formation that is located above Jerome, is also found thousands of feet lower in elevation along the Verde River near Sycamore Canyon.

Numerous faults throughout the Sedona area were formed as the Verde Valley expanded. The Dry Creek Fault is clearly evident where a vertical line separates the Supai Sandstone from the House Mountain basalt in a road cut just to the west of the bridge over Dry Creek on SR 89A at mile- post 366.

Fault Line

The Dry Creek Fault in a road cut on SR 89A at Milepost 366 is one example of the many faults throughout the Sedona area

The Creation of the Verde Formation

The Essentials

Formation Name: Verde Formation
Rock Type: Limestone and conglomerate formed
                of rim gravels from erosion sediment
                deposition.
Time Frame: 6 a.m. December 31st to present, over
                the past 8 million years
Era: Middle Cenozoic, Age of Mammals
Life Forms: First sign of early man and whales
Location: High desert basin
Latitude: North of the equator
Aver. Thickness: 3,000 to 5,000 feet
Best Viewed: The gray hills south and west of Clark-
                dale

As the low point at the base of the Mogollon Highlands, the Ancestral Verde Valley already contained a considerable amount of eroded materials from the slopes above. When the Verde Valley faulted downward, it became the lowest point of a very large drainage area. Rivers flowing into the valley filled it with gravels deposited from the both the eroding Mogollon Highlands to the southwest, and the Colorado Plateau to the northwest.

Water trapped in the Verde Valley formed a vast inland fresh water lake. As the size of the Verde Lake intermittently expanded and shrank within the valley, layers of mudstone, sandstone and limestone were deposited. This gives the Verde Formation a "banded look" where limestone layers alternate with rocky conglomerate, sandstone and mudstone. Calcium from the limestone leached into the erosion debris layers below cementing the gravels into layers of conglomerate.

As the Ancestral Verde River flowed through the valley during dry periods, it eroded away massive amounts of the Verde Formation reforming the valley. Then approximately 4.8 million years ago, enormous Rim Basalt flows flowed through Sycamore Canyon and into the Verde Valley. Then as the Verde Lake expanded during wet periods, limestone deposits of the Verde Formation covered the basalts. In recent times the Verde River has once more eroded away the younger Verde Formation deposits and has cut down through the

The Verde Formation looking west from the smelter in Clarkdale. The formation is comprised primarily of fresh water limestones from the inland seas that filled the valley supplemented with conglomerate and river gravels washed down from the Colorado Plateau and the Mogollon Highlands.

Rim Basalt flows that filled the valley, forming a basalt canyon and giving the valley its sculpted look of today.

Along the Verde Canyon Railroad for the first five miles of the excursion from Clarkdale, the Verde River has cut down through a basalt lava flow, forming a 150 foot vertical-walled basalt canyon. A good place to see this canyon is from the SOB Bridge on the railway. Past the SOB Bridge, other different distinct lava flows deposited early in the valley's formation can be seen.

Basalt

Schnebly Hill Formation

Verde Formation

Supai Group

Basalt

A view of the rock formations lining the Verde Valley

The Verde Canyon Railroad travels 150 feet above the Verde River as it flows through a
basalt canyon near the SOB Bridge

Chapter 10

The Finishing Touches: *Carving Oak Creek Canyon and the Eruption of the San Francisco Volcanic Field*

(Noon to the Present, December 31, 6 Million Years Ago to Present)

Oak Creek Canyon

The Essentials

Formation Name: Oak Creek Canyon
Time Frame: 8 a.m. to Noon, December 31st to present, 8 to 6 million years ago
Era: Middle Cenozoic, Age of Mammals
Life Forms: First sign of early man and whales
Location: High desert basin of the modern world
Latitude: North of the equator
Size: Dropping approximately 1,000 feet along 18 miles
Best Viewed: SR 89A through Oak Creek Canyon At the scenic overlook at the top of the switchbacks

Some 80 million years ago when the Rocky Mountains were being formed, a 30-mile long fault was created running from Sedona to Flagstaff and the San Francisco Peaks. The east side of the Fault was raised up more than 600 feet above the west side.

Water seeking weak spots in Earth's crust carved out the Ancestral Oak Creek Canyon. River rock and gravels from the river that flowed through the canyon can be found on the top of the 300-foot high Airport Mesa in Sedona.

The Oak Creek Fault separates Wilson Mountain and Wilson Bench

Then about noon on December 31st, 8 to 6 million years ago, massive amounts of basalt lava flowed into the Verde River drainage from high up on the Colorado Plateau. Wilson Mountain above Sedona was a cinder cone volcano during this period. Lavas from Wilson Mountain completely filled the Ancestral Oak Creek Canyon and covered the Sedona area. Evidence of these lava flows can be viewed on the tops of Wilson and Munds Mountains, Schnebly Hill and the cliff walls in Oak Creek Canyon.

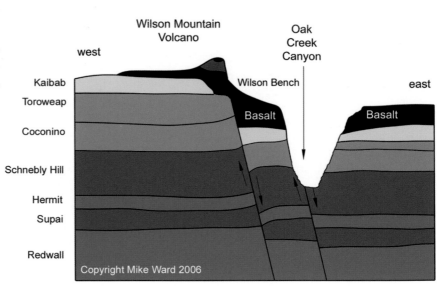

Basalt and the broken cinder cone on the top of Wilson Mountain and Wilson Bench along the fault lines in Oak Creek Canyon

The gradual uplifting of the Colorado Plateau has lifted the plateau over 2,500 feet during the past six million years. The Oak Creek Fault deep in Earth's surface became active again, fracturing the basalt fill in the Ancestral Oak Creek Canyon. Evidence of this second faulting is clearly visible where the fault line divides the old Wilson Mountain cinder cone from what is known as Wilson Mountain Bench to the east pictured on the previous page. The bench was dropped 836 feet below the level of Wilson Mountain. The east side of the canyon was dropped an additional 160 feet making the total displacement between the east and west sides of the canyon over 1,000 feet.

Over the past 6 million years, Oak Creek has been carving the Modern Oak Creek Canyon we see today. Abandoning its original channel over the Airport Mesa, it has alternately channeled on either side of the mesa. The creek flows on the south side of the mesa today. Carroll Canyon gives testimony to the abandoned creek channel on the north side of the mesa.

The 980-year old volcano named Sunset Crater near Flagstaff

The San Francisco Volcanic Field

The Essentials

Formation Name: San Francisco Volcanic Field
Time Frame: Noon, December 31st to present, 6 million years ago
Era: Middle Cenozoic, Age of Mammals
Life Forms: First sign of early man and whales
Location: High desert basin of the modern world
Latitude: North of the equator
Size: Over 600 volcanic ash cones along a 50-mile swath
Best Viewed: Sunset Crater National Monument
San Francisco Peaks

As the Oak Creek Fault was forming Oak Creek Canyon, there was considerable volcanic activity to the north in the Flagstaff area. In addition to the 2,500 foot uplift of the Colorado Plateau over the past six million years, the Plateau has also moved westward over 50 miles. A localized "hot spot" of magma was formed near Earth's surface. Periodically, volcanoes have erupted from this hot spot forming an area known as the San Francisco Volcanic Field. The western most volcano and also the oldest (approximately six million years old) in this field is Williams Mountain near Williams, Arizona.

As the North American Plate moved over the stationary hot spot, new volcanoes periodically formed. There are over 600 volcanoes in the volcanic field. On average, a new volcano was formed every 10,000 years. The youngest volcano (approximately 980 years old) is Sunset Crater, located to the east of Flagstaff.

By far the largest of the volcanoes was the 16,000-foot high San Francisco Volcano above Flagstaff. About 440,000 years ago, the volcano exploded in a catastrophic volcanic blast perhaps 100 times as violent as the Mount St. Helen eruption in 1990. The topmost four thousand feet of the volcano were strewn around the entire Four Corners area. Volcanic bombs, molten lava that cools and becomes solid while flying through the air, ranging from softball-sized to house-sized, rained down over the Flagstaff area.

Nearly 4,000 feet of the San Francisco Volcano summit exploded 440,000 years ago

A 16,000-foot volcano formed the San Francisco Peaks above Flagstaff

Erosional forces are forming two adjoining arches near the Soldier Pass Trail. This view shows the formation of one of the arches below and the light coming down from above through the crevice opening.

Chapter 11

Sedona's Natural Arches, Sinkholes and Desert Varnish:
What Are They and How Were They Formed?

Sedona's Natural Arches

A natural arch or bridge is a rock formation where a narrow ridge forms with an open natural passageway underneath. The distinction between a "natural arch" and a "natural bridge" is somewhat arbitrary. Typically, arches have rounded tops while bridges are flat on the top.

Sandstone lends itself to the formation of natural arches. Horizontal layers of sediments called bedding planes characterize the sedimentary sandstones around Sedona. Over the millenniums, movements of the earth's crust have fractured the layered sandstone vertically. As erosional forces work on the sandstones, the vertical cracks widen into crevasses and the horizontal bedding planes wear away to form shallow caves. Eventually these erosional forces cause the formation of a natural bridge.

A classic example of this process can be observed in the Schnebly Hill Sandstone Formation in the walls of Brins Ridge off the Soldier Pass Trail. There, a fifteen-foot thick slab of cliff face has separated from a vertical rock formation. The crevass that separates the rock slab from the parent sandstone cliff ranges from several inches to several feet in width. Two adjoining hollows, or shallow caves, have formed in the lower bedding planes in the base of the separating ridge. By walking to the back of the shallow caves, it is possible to peer upward and see the sky through the crevass. As erosion widens the gap between the separated rock slab and the parent cliff wall, two adjoining natural arches will be formed.

Another example of a natural arch is in Fay Canyon above and to the east of the Fay Canyon Trail. This arch appears to have been formed in the same manner as the Soldier Pass arches. The separation of the arch from the cliff face is about twelve feet and the top of the ridge has eroded below the elevation of the parent cliff formation. From a distance, the arch appears to be a shallow cave in the cliff face. After

Looking up from underneath Fay Canyon Arch through the crevice separating the arch from the adjoining cliff face

The arches off the Solder Pass Trail are early in their formative stage

Fay Canyon Arch is evident as one sees the daylight entering the slot behind the forming arch

A fully formed arch, Vultee Arch is located approximately two miles down the Vultee Arch Trail

Looking through Devil's Bridge at the end of the 0.7-mile long Devil's Bridge Trail

climbing up to the formation and walking into the shallow cave and looking upward at the sky, the formation of the arch is obvious.

Vultee Arch on the Vultee Arch Trail and Devil's Bridge at the end of the Devil's Bridge Trail are both examples of mature natural arches. Both are easily accessible from their respective trails. Devil's Bridge may be classified as a natural bridge because the top of the arch is relatively flat.

Sedona's Sinkholes

Sinkholes are common in areas where the rock formation below the land surface is limestone or other rocks that can be dissolved by ground water circulating through them. As slightly acidic ground water dissolves the Redwall Limestone beneath Sedona, underground spaces and caverns are formed.

As the dissolved spaces and caverns grow larger, natural faults and structural weaknesses in the rock formations above the Redwall Limestone can cause the formations to pancake down into the cavity exposing a 1,000 foot deep sinkhole on the surface. Devil's Kitchen on the Soldier Pass Trail and Devil's Dining Room on the Broken Arrow Trail are two examples of the many sinkholes around Sedona.

Reportedly, local settlers witnessed the formation of Devil's Kitchen in 1880, when they were startled by a tremendous thundering sound accompanied by a massive cloud of dust. The sinkhole is approximately 150 feet across and perhaps 80 feet deep. The massive rock at the back of the sinkhole broke free of the overlying rock in the early 1970's.

At approximately 30 feet across and 80 feet deep, Devil's Dining Room is a smaller but equally

Resting on the top of a 1,000 foot deep pile of debris, the large block of rock at the back of Devil's Kitchen on the Soldier Pass Trail collapsed into the sinkhole in the early 1970's

Devil's Dining Room located on the Broken Arrow Trail, is a habitat for bats. The sinkhole
is protected by a wire fence to discourage people from repelling down into the sinkhole and
disturbing the bat colony that lives there

impressive sinkhole that is also a bat habitat. When looking into the sinkholes, visitors are looking at the top of rock rubble that extends downward perhaps a thousand feet, through the Schnebly Hill Sandstone, Hermit Shale, and Supai Group, into the Redwall Limestone.

Black desert vanish streaks down the north face of Sedona's famous Cathedral Rock

Desert Varnish

Desert varnish is common throughout the arid desert regions of the Southwest. Desert varnish is a thin patina, only one-hundredth of a millimeter thick, that can color entire rock wall cliffs black or reddish-brown. The desert varnish found in the Sedona area is on the Schnebly Hill Formation sandstone cliffs.

As rain and run-off waters flow down the rock surfaces, the water reacts with the manganese and iron oxide in the fine-grained clay materials within the sandstone to form a manganese oxide. Microscopic organisms of bacteria colonize the manganese oxide. The bacteria absorb trace amounts of manganese oxide and iron oxide from the rock and precipitate it as a black or reddish film on the rock surfaces. This thin layer also includes cemented clay particles that help shield the bacteria against intense solar radiation. As the organisms live and die over the course of as long as a thousand years, the desert varnish thickens, becoming more pronounced.

Desert varnish plays an important role in deciphering the culture of the ancient Sinagua Indians who thrived around Sedona for a thousand years before leaving the area about 700 years ago. The Sinagua carved petroglyphs in the black patina of the desert varnish where the underlying red sandstone would contrast with the black coating.

Around Sedona, there are Sinagua petroglyph sites at Palatki, Honanki, and V - Bar - V heritage sites. Among the hundreds of petroglyphs at the V - Bar - V site is a recently interpreted Solar Calendar used by the Sinagua to determine planting and harvesting times for their various crops. Kenneth Zoll, who first observed the solar calendar, has published a book, *Sinagua Sunwatchers* documenting the shafts of sunlight that pass over a series of petroglyphs only on certain days of the year to mark the planting and harvesting days. The proceeds of this book go to Sedona's Friends of the Forest, a service group supporting the Red Rock Ranger District of the Coconino National Forest, the book's public education web site and to the Verde Valley Archaeological Society.

Kenneth Zoll, an archeological site volunteer docent for Sedona's Friends of the Forest, spent a year documenting the alignment of these petroglyphs at V - Bar - V , to demonstrate how the Sinagua Indians used them as a solar calendar to determine planting and harvesting times. The proceeds of this book go to Sedona's Friends of the Forest, the book's public education web site and to the Verde Valley Archaeological Society.

In Conclusion

Sedona is a place of unparalleled natural beauty. The attraction to the red rock formations felt by residents and visitors alike has an almost mystical quality about it. Sedona is a unique and extraordinary place.

It should not be surprising that Sedona has a geologic history that is perhaps the most interesting in North America. All the ingredients for a fascinating geologic story are here. Massive, ancient and relatively young volcanoes spread their lavas here. Major deposits of gold, silver and copper were formed near here. Great faulting events have created valleys and canyons around Sedona.

There has been vertical uplifting of large plates without disturbing the underlying formations to the north. Mountain-building that chaotically broke up the underlying formations occurred to the south of Sedona. Finally, an almost unimaginable amount of erosion has removed literally miles of sedimentary rock from over the Sedona area, and then further erosion sculpted the red rock formations that we see in Sedona today.

Considering the vastness of time it took to produce the geology that is Sedona, the almost unimaginable magnitude of the forces that were involved, and the extraordinary combination of geologic events that created Sedona, it is no wonder that Sedona is a place like no other.

Sedona from Munds Mountain looking westward

Bibliography

Kring,   David A., 2002. *Desert Heat and Volcanic Fire*, Tucson, AZ, Arizona Geologic Society.

Mathis,   Allyson and Carl Bowman, Spring 2005. "What's in a Number" *Nature Notes*, Grand Canyon National Park, Volume XXI, Number 2

Ranney,   Wayne D. R., 2001. *Sedona Through Time - Geology of the Red Rocks*, Flagstaff, AZ: Zia Interpretative Services.

Ranney,   Wayne D. R., 1989. *The Verde Valley - A Geologic History*, Flagstaff, AZ: Plateau Magazine, Museum of Northern Arizona.

Wiewandt, Thomas and Wilks, Maureen, 2004. *The Southwest Insideout*, Tucson, AZ: Wild Horzons Publishing.

BBC Learning information, Mass Extinction Events, a good introduction to Earth's mass extinction events

> http://www.bbc.co.uk/education/darwin/exfiles/massintro.htm

Geology and Geophysics, University of Calgary, Discussion of geologic time

> http://www.geo.ucalgary.ca/~macrae/timescale/timescale.html

Plate Tectonics, a historical perspective, USGS, Basic discussion on plate tectonics

> http://pubs.usgs.gov/publications/text/historical.html

Scotese, Christopher R., PALEOMAP Project, Excellent visual aids on plate tectonics
http://www.scotese.com/Default.htm

Western Region Geologic Information, USGS, Basic geologic information on the southwest

> http://wrgis.wr.usgs.gov/

Wikipedia, the free encyclopedia: Earth, An excellent background on the Earth

> http://en.wikipedia.org/wiki/Earth

Wikipedia, the free encyclopedia: Plate Tectonics, Basic discussion on plate tectonics

> http://en.wikipedia.org/wiki/Plate_tectonics

Wikipedia, the free encyclopedia: Laramide Orogeny, Discussion of the uplifting of the Southwest

> http://en.wikipedia.org/wiki/Laramide_orogeny

Glossary of Common Geologic Terms

Basalt: A fine-grained igneous rock relatively high in manganese and iron and low in silica formed from the rapid cooling of lava at the surface or in thin intrusions. Basalt is the most common rock on the earth's surface.

Butte: A step-sided mesa whose height is nearly the same or more than its diameter or length.

Caldera: The depression formed after the dome of a volcano collapses downward into the void created by lavas that flowed out of the volcano.

Chert: A very hard, smooth, sedimentary rock cemented by silicate. Its hardness and tendency to break with sharp edges made it useful for prehistoric cutting tools and weapon points.

Conglomerate: A sedimentary rock formed from rounded gravels cemented together by another mineral substance. The size and composition of the included gravels may be extremely variable within one specimen of conglomerate. The rock is usually found in the location of ancient streambeds. If the gravel fragments are angular rather than rounded, it is called breccia.

Contact: The plane where two faulted formations or members meet.

Cross-bedding: Structure in which rock forms from depositions having slope and causing thin layers of rock to be inclined at an angle rather than horizontal. It is usually found in sandstone preserving the leeward slope of wind-blown sand dunes.

Desert varnish: Caused by water reacting to the manganese in sandstones. The manganese oxides create habitats for bacteria colonies that form a blackened surface on rock faces over a thousand years.

Dike: An igneous flow (lava) which solidified in a vertical rock fissure.

Dolomite: A sedimentary rock similar to limestone but with higher magnesium content.

Extrusive rock: Igneous rock formed from the rapid cooling of lava on the earth's surface resulting in a fine crystal structure (example: basalt).

Fault: A fracture in a rock mass caused by compression or tension along which there has been relative movement that may be vertical, horizontal or a combination.

Formation: One or more stratum of rock formed in a single period in essentially the same environment.

Fracture: A crack or break in a rock formation along which there has been no appreciable movement (also referred to as a "fissure").

Geology: The youngest of the sciences. It involves the study of the earth's structure, composition and the changes which have occurred and are occurring.

Igneous rock: Any rock formed by the crystallization of molten magma (examples: granite, basalt).

Intrusive rock: Igneous rock that formed below the earth's surface and, therefore, cooled slowly, forming crystals of significant size (example: granite).

Inverted topography: A condition where an erosion-resistant rock originally deposited at a lower elevation is now elevated relative to its surroundings due to differential erosion of softer surrounding rock (such as the mesa tops near the Village of Oak Creek).

Lava: Molten rock (magma) which reaches the earth's surface.

Limestone: A sedimentary rock formed by the deposition of calcium carbonate from solution originating either directly from dissolved marine skeletons or from re-dissolved limestone.

Lithification: The process of compaction and cementation, usually by calcite or silicate, of sediments to form solid rock.

Magma: Subterranean molten rock (called lava if reaches the surface).

Member: A sub-group of a formation representing a different rock type or minor differences in the environment of deposition.

Mesa: An eroded landform having a relatively flat top and steep sides due to an erosion-resistant cap rock and whose height is substantially less than its diameter or length.

Metamorphic rock: Solid rock altered in its crystalline structure by heat and pressure (examples: quartzite from sandstone, marble from limestone, slate from shale).

Mineral: A naturally occurring inorganic solid composed of a single element or of a compound and having a definite crystal structure and composition.

Mudstone: A sedimentary rock formed from the lithification of clay and mud deposited under turbulent water conditions ("shale" if under calm conditions).

mya: An abbreviation for "millions of years ago."

Obsidian: Black, volcanic glass formed when fluid, high silica content lava is cooled nearly instantaneously by immersion in water, thus preventing the formation of crystals (not naturally occurring in the Sedona area).

Pangaea: Meaning "all land," the name given to the single earth land mass existing from about 320 mya until its breakup into continents about 200 mya.

Pinnacle (spire): An eroded landmass whose height is many times its diameter.

Plate Tectonics: The movement of plates of continental and oceanic crust over the earth's mantle.

Rock: A solid material composed of a single mineral or of several minerals that are cemented or fused together rather than chemically bonded.

Sandstone: A sedimentary rock composed predominately of lithified quartz (sand) grains.

Sedimentary rock: Rock formed from lithification of the weathered products of pre-existing rocks (for examples: sandstone, shale) or solidified from solution (examples: limestone, chert).

Shale: A usually fragile sedimentary rock formed by the lithification of layers of clay or mud deposited under calm water conditions ("mudstone" if under turbulent conditions).

Shield volcano: A broad, gently sloping volcano built from the non-violent flow of fluid basaltic lava (examples: House Mountain, Mormon Mountain).

Siltstone: A sedimentary rock formed from the lithification of silt deposits.

Sinkhole: A depression formed by the dissolving of a soluble rock (such as limestone, dolomite or halite) below the surface, resulting in a cave-in of the ground above (local examples: Devil's Kitchen and Devil's Dining Room).

Sorting: The degree of uniformity of particle size in sedimentary rock.

Stratum (pl., strata): A layer of sedimentary rock having its own characteristics.

Unconformity: A contact surface between two adjacent rock layers of different ages representing a break in the rock record caused by a period of erosion or non-deposition.

Vesicles: Voids created in lava rock due to the presence of gas bubbles during solidification.